# The Getaway Chef

Make your getaway cooking terrific—instead of terrify-
ing. Now you need pack no more than a head of garlic,
a couple of lemons and your copy of **The Getaway Chef**.
Jane Rodmell and Kate Bush tell you how to stock
your pantry (with ingredients that are readily available at
even the most basic country store) and equip your
kitchen, to make it easy for you to leave town in a hurry
and enjoy good food far from the city's conveniences.
Here are favourite recipes, friendly advice and dozens of
tips to make holiday cooking a pleasure instead of a chore.

# THE GETAWAY CHEF

## Great Food For the Cook on Holiday

Jane Rodmell and Kate Bush

KEY PORTER BOOKS

CANADIAN CATALOGUING IN PUBLICATION
DATA

Rodmell, Jane, 1938-
    The getaway chef

Includes index.
ISBN 0-919493-04-1

1. Outdoor cookery. 2. Cookery. I. Bush, Kate,
1948-
II. Title.

TX823.R62       641.5'78       C83-098378-3

Illustrations by Judy Tarves
Designed by Ken Rodmell

Printed and bound in Canada

## Acknowledgments

Our warmest thanks to our families and
the many friends who helped and
encouraged us during the making of
this book: Judy Tarves, who gave
generously of her talents and delighted
us with her drawings; Debbie Davidson,
Helen Skwarok and Dave and Mary
Bush who tested, tasted and passed
judgement on the recipes; Carol Sale,
who cheerfully deciphered illegible
handwriting and endured marathon
typing sessions; and especially, John
and Ken, our husbands, who nobly
tolerate mildewing lettuce in the car,
chaos in the kitchen and books and
papers everywhere.

J.R. & K.B.

# Contents

# Introduction

Two things should be avoided in life, bad temper and indigestion
*X. Marcel Boulestin*

... especially on holiday.
*Jane and Kate*

**W**e believe that most of us, while out of town for a weekend or a week, would rather sail, snorkel, terrorize the slopes, or just soak up the sun than labour in the kitchen. However, whether you holiday in a condo in Florida, a ski chalet in Utah or a cottage in northern Ontario, you still have to eat.

Time after time we have set out from the city with the car trunk jammed with a hastily gathered, sometimes quite extraordinary, collection of food stuffs. Sometimes the chance to escape the city's frenzy presents itself only at 5 o'clock on a Friday evening; very often friends are asked to come along at the last minute. Add to that our fondness for eating well and it is clear that we needed to organize ourselves.

When you get right down to it, this cookbook has arisen out of necessity.

What we needed was a little book, an 'aide memoire', where everything was written down, so that in the last minute rush to get away we would not have to think. It would have lists of those essential things that we should never be without; it would help us out in emergencies when we were about to feed eight unexpected guests; it would provide a selection of dishes which could be prepared ahead of time, perhaps stored in the freezer, and taken along; and it would remind us how to make those easy, favourite things collected over the years from grandmothers and friends who are good cooks. We wanted it all collected in one place, never to be lost, misplaced or forgotten—all those neat tricks, short cuts and helpful hints which, in our experience, have worked to make preparing good food on holiday a pleasure and never a chore.

The recipes in this book are, for the most part, quick and easy to make and require only basic skill with pots and pans. To prepare them, the cook needs only the simplest collection of cooking equipment and a relatively small number of familiar ingredients, the bulk of which can be found even in a remote country store.

If you want to enjoy good food at the holiday place, the only things you may really need to tuck into your tote bag are a head of garlic, a couple of lemons and a copy of **The Getaway Chef**.

# The Getaway Kitchen

It's no wonder many people find cooking frustrating. They use pots so thin everything burns, knives so dull cutting one carrot is a feat for Superman and frying pans so pitted they act like glue on fried eggs. We used to think almost no equipment was necessary in a kitchen. In fact, one of us spent an entire summer cooking with one frying pan, which doubled as a serving dish, and a dull knife. Now we realize that good equipment is not only useful but it is the key to easy cooking.

Here's a guide to help you sort through the overwhelming kitchen battery. We have singled out the cookware and tools we use most frequently in our permanent holiday kitchen, and with these items you will be able to prepare every dish included in the book.

## Essential Cookware

**Large Pot:** A typical scenario portrays the frustrated cook trying to push a pound of spaghetti into a one-quart pot. The spaghetti sticks, the water boils over and the cook goes mad. Have a large pot, 8 to 10 quart (7 to 9L) size, which is tall instead of wide and, therefore, fits the circumference of the stove burner better. One of enamelled steel or aluminum will do just fine, or even a canning pot. The latter is thin on the bottom and not suitable for browning meats or vegetables, but it is certainly adequate for simmering soups, boiling pasta or the occasional lobster, and reheating stews. A restaurant supply house is the ideal place to shop for these.

**Another Large Pot:** This one should be of a solid material, 3-ply stainless steel, heavy-gauge aluminum, cast-iron or porcelain-enamelled cast-iron, wider and shallower than the other, about 6-quart (5L) size. In it large batches of meat can be browned at one time for all the braised meat and stew-type dishes. Ours is of well-seasoned cast-iron which cooks well on top of the stove and in the oven. It is just deep enough to hold a whole chicken or a four pound pot roast. The material is dense and the lid fits well so that it acts like a slow-cooker—a pot of chili or pork and beans can be left in a low oven to cook away all day and will still emerge moist and tender.

**The Saucepan:** We often come across the 'I hate to cook' person trying to make a white sauce in a pot that looks like a bomb hit it because someone has used it as a hammer to fix the pump. Invest in two solid saucepans with tight-fitting lids (3-ply stainless steel or heavy-gauge aluminium will do nicely). One about 1½-quart (1.5L) size and the other about 3-quart (3L) size should be adequate for all occasions.

If you need a **double boiler:** Set an inch (2.5 cm) or so of water simmering in the larger saucepan and use a bowl which fits snuggly in the pan just above the water.

If you need a **steamer:** Set a sieve over simmering water in the large saucepan and cover.

If you need a **deep fryer:** Heat oil in the large heavy pot and use a slotted spoon to remove the fried food.

**Skillet or Frying Pan:** A heavy solid 12" (29 cm) skillet will serve as a pot, sauté pan and baking dish, as long as the handle is ovenproof. Our favourite is of cast-iron—we picked it up in a junk shop for a few dollars. It is beautifully blackened with a satin-smooth finish which acts like the non-stick variety, and it may be used in the oven. (Just don't grab the handle with your bare hands when you remove the skillet from a hot oven.)

To season a new iron skillet: Fill the pan with oil to ½" (1.25 cm) from the top. Heat the oil just to smoking point, then turn heat to low and leave for an hour. Pour off the oil (it may be reused) and wipe the pan with paper towels. Now use it! That's the real secret. If your frying pan just sits on the shelf, it will soon lose its finish.

A cover for the pan is essential. If the frying pan doesn't come with one, try the lid from your large pot, or use foil in a pinch.

**Second frying pan** about 10" (25 cm), with a non-stick surface is handy for cooking eggs and creamed sauces, and if you find yourself often cooking for a crowd, the giant electric griddle with a non-stick surface will be handy.

**Roasting Pan:** A large shallow pan (about 17" x 12" x 2"/42 cm x 28 cm x 5 cm) can be used in the oven for everything from Lemon Potatoes to the Thanksgiving turkey. If it has a rack, you can use it to grill steaks, fish, etc. Also use the rack to turn out cakes and cool cookies.

**Oven Cookware:** For cooking in the oven use equipment which is solid and versatile. The basic list would include **two shallow baking pans**, 8" x 8" x 2" (2L) and 9" x 13" x 2" (3L) of ovenproof glass, earthenware, stoneware, non-stick steel or enamelled cast-iron; **one loaf pan**, 9" x 5" (2L) non-stick steel; **muffin tin** for 12 muffins with deep cups; **cookie sheet**, 11" x 17" (29 cm x 44 cm) (if you are a serious cookie maker have two or more cookie sheets then the baking process is quick and easy). Make sure you buy solid, not thin and flimsy ones. Use them also for making pizzas; **pie plate**, 9" (1L) diameter, ovenproof glass is best for all-purpose use. It looks fine on the table and can double as a gratin dish for chicken, fish and vegetables.

## Essential Tools

**Large Colander:** The following is an all too familiar occurrence. You, the cook, are trying to strain the water from a large pot of pasta with one small strainer in hand. The steam burns your forearm and fogs your vision, but you're determined not to let go. One slippery noodle sneaks over the side. The rest follows immediately and you end up staring with dismay at a sink full of pasta. Equip yourself with a large, strong colander.

**Small Strainer:** Made of fine stainless-steel mesh about 7" (18 cm) in diameter is useful to smoothen a lumpy sauce or to use as a flour sifter.

**Knives:** If we had only one knife in the kitchen, it would be a chef's knife with an 8" (19 cm) blade with a good sharp edge. Usually the lower-priced line of a well-known brand is a good bet. The second knife would be a razor-sharp paring knife with a 3" to 4" (8 cm to 10 cm) blade.

**A Peeler:** When the blade dulls, throw it out and buy a new one at once. It costs very little.

**Measuring Cups:** If there's one thing that can lay waste the joy of cooking, it's having to constantly wash out measuring cups, or worse still trying to make do with an old teacup. We suggest you invest in 3 sizes of measuring cups: 1 cup, 2 cup and 4 cup (metric sizes: 250 mL, 500 mL, and 1L); made of transparent ovenproof glass or plastic. It's wise, although not essential, to have a second set of measuring cups: a stacking set of stainless steel in ¼, ⅓, ½ and 1 cup sizes (metric sizes: 50 mL, 125 mL and 250 mL) for measuring dry ingredients.

**Measuring Spoons:** We have got by with a pinch (⅛ teaspoon/.5 mL), a dash and a sprinkle (¼ teaspoon/1 mL) and a good squeeze (one tablespoon/ 15 mL), but there are times when accuracy must prevail, especially in baking. We recommend you use a set of measuring spoons in ¼ teaspoon, ½ teaspoon, 1 teaspoon and 1 tablespoon sizes (metric measure: 1 mL, 2 mL, 5 mL, 15 mL and 25 mL). Choose spoons with oval rather than deep round bowls. They are easier to clean.

**Chopping Board:** Many of us have faced the scourge of the too small chopping block—bits of onion flying in every direction or the vegetables for the soup ending up on the floor rather than in the pot. The simplest chopping board is a piece of hardwood left over from building the dock or veranda. Sand it well and wipe with vegetable oil. Use one side for onions and garlic and the other for bread and pastry. Mark the corner of the bread side with a 'B' so you won't forget which side is which.

**Can Opener:** Buy yourself a serious can opener: not an electric gadget but a good solid hand model.

**Grater:** The old-fashioned metal box grater does a good job. One side has smooth-edged holes for grating cheese, carrots and apples. Two sides have rough edges for grating orange rind or nutmeg. The fourth side slices.

**Blender:** If banana daiquiris aren't an essential part of your diet, you can probably live without a blender, but it is very useful. If you have to do without, here are a few options:

- Make the recipe ahead and take it along.
- Use a wire strainer and push the food through with the back of a spoon.
- Buy a food mill. It looks a little like part of the space shuttle, but with almost no effort you can mash or purée many things.

**Juicer:** The old-fashioned heavy glass juicer has a handle to steady it, a deep ridge to hold the juice and a spout to pour the juice out. To extract juice from citrus fruit have fruit at room temperature. Press and roll it on a counter to break down the fibers. Cut in half crosswise and jab the open edge with the tines of a fork.

**Hand or Electric Beater:** There have been many times at the ski chalet and the cottage when someone has had to beat cream for Irish coffee with a whisk. Boring! A simple three-speed portable electric mixer does the job in no time and is invaluable for blending butter and sugar, if you enjoy baking cakes and cookies.

**Whisk:** Use for eggs or on the occasion when whipping must be done by hand. Choose one with fine stainless-steel wires securely attached to a strong, metal handle of a size to fit your mixing bowl.

**Bowls:** Make sure you have at least two sizes—medium sized, about 1½ quart (1.5 L), and a large mixing bowl, 4 quarts (4 L), made of glass, stainless steel or heavy plastic.

**Rolling Pin:** Good to have on hand. If not, a bottle will work in a pinch or so will a rolling pin made of a large dowel, at least 20" cm long, sanded smooth and rubbed well with vegetable oil.

**Salad Dryer:** For years washing all the green stuff for salads and patting it dry was a real chore. The spinning plastic salad dryer takes away the drudgery and for us it is essential.

**Wooden Spoons:** You will need two. One long-handled with an oval bowl for stirring soups and stews, and one flat for blending butter and sauces.

**Spatulas:** Two with flat rubber tips. You'll need the extra one since chances are you'll leave one too near the stove burner and the tip will melt. One long-handled with a perforated blade for turning hamburgers, draining fried foods and removing cookies from the baking tray. A long narrow flexible type works best.

**Slotted Spoon:** Useful for lifting out poached eggs and removing fried foods from hot oil.

**Potato Masher:** As long as you can convince someone else to use it.

**Skewers:** Toothpicks, 9" (23 cm) wooden skewers ideal for grilled snacks and appetizers, and large metal ones for shish kabobs.

Finally, **a corkscrew:** To open the wine to sip while preparing a few snacks from The Happy Hour!

The following gadgets are not essential but are fun and useful to have:

**Melon Baller**

**Egg Slicer**

**Cheese Slicer**

**Wok:** Ideal for deep frying, sautéing, steaming, stewing.

**Ice Cream Scoop:** Get the kind with alcohol in the handle. This keeps the ice cream from sticking.

**Scallop Shells:** These make great serving dishes for appetizers, salads, even desserts.

**Mallet:** For the hunter in the family; to pound venison or moose.

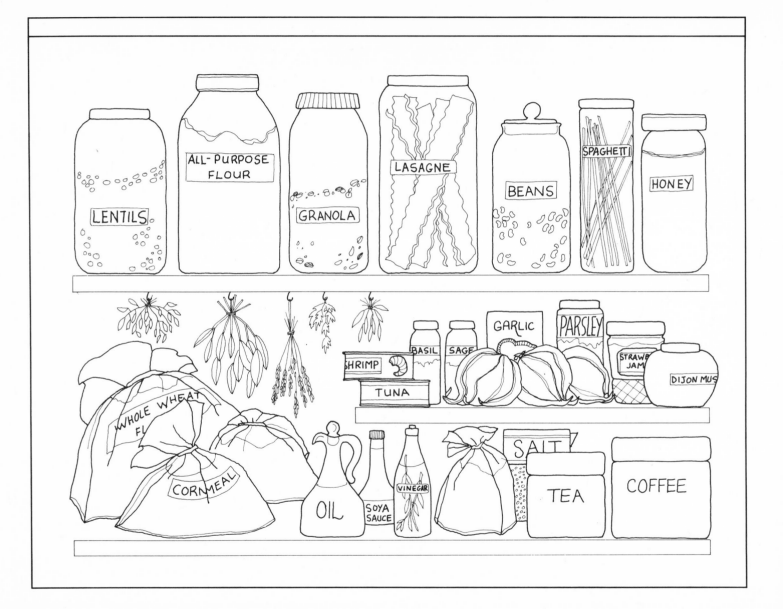

# The Store Cupboard

If you want to enjoy good food away from home, there is no alternative but to plan a little. For years we have made spontaneous flights from the city, only to realize halfway to our destination that we have forgotten the butter. Or we arrive to find there are six packages of spaghetti in the cupboard and no tomatoes (and, of course, back in the city we have six cans of tomatoes and no spaghetti). In the rush to leave we neglect to check the refrigerator one last time and we set off without the cheese and the salad fixings, the lovingly prepared ratatouille or the marinating shish kabobs.

We have prepared the list of all lists to help you avoid frustrating times like these. We suggest you use it as a checklist on your shopping trips.

If you have your own permanent holiday place, you can keep a well-stocked cupboard of non-perishables and make getting away in a hurry that much simpler. These items also come in handy when the boat motor breaks down again or six friends pay an unexpected visit. Remember to transfer the contents of packages and bags into large glass or tin containers with well-fitting lids to guard against pests and dampness. One winter a particularly single-minded Muskoka mouse removed twenty-five pounds of dog-food, piece by piece, into winter storage. We opened the door of the medicine cabinet to be met with an avalanche of dog chow. Our shelves are lined with giant peanut butter jars and large preserving jars filled with grains, nuts and dried fruit, and we have found that the local restaurant supply house is a good source for sturdy plastic containers with good lids in a wide range of sizes—useful for cereals, flour, sugar, pet food and such.

If you are spending time in borrowed or rented places, the best plan of attack is to decide what you would like to eat for each meal and plan accordingly, even going so far as to prepare ahead a number of main dishes or some sweet treats to take along. When you have to travel light, measure out the estimated amounts of ingredients you will use into small, plastic bags, tied securely and labelled if necessary. On trips like these we make extensive use of the items in our Useful Shortcut list.

The items listed in bold type comprise the basic store cupboard from which most of the recipes in this book can be prepared. Those listed in regular type are essential in a few special-occasion favourite dishes. We list them so they will be included in your shopping list should these dishes become your favourites too.

## Secret Store Cupboard

If you want to whip up great-tasting meals in the wilderness with a minimum of fuss there are a few tricks you can have up your sleeve (i.e. in the storecupboard). Your friends will consider you a genius—Julia Child no less!

Splurge on a good brand of premium **olive oil** (light and fragrant, not one which is overpowering in texture or taste) and two good vinegars, a **tarragon-flavoured white wine vinegar** and a more robust **red wine vinegar**. Avoid those in plastic bottles because they seem to develop an unpleasant, chemical taste. Have on hand a splendid **Dijon-style mustard** to use as a flavouring and as a condiment and serve **fine butter** and **great coffee**. A jar of **real maple syrup, home-made style preserves** and **chili sauce** is always a hit too. **Freshly grated imported Parmesan cheese** is in another world from the common packaged kind. (This, like coffee, maintains more flavour when kept in a sealed container in the freezer. Bring to room temperature when needed.)

If you have a sunny spot close to the holiday place, plant a small clump of **chives**, **mint** and **parsley** this spring.

# Perishables

Perishable items should be picked up for each trip and any leftovers should be lugged home again. The alternative is organisms rampant in the refrigerator by the time of your next visit.

## FROM THE BUTCHER

Many of the main dish recipes in this book are adaptable to more than one variety of meat. Your choice, naturally, will be determined by what is available and good at the market. Keep in mind that meat, when ground or cubed, travels less well than meat still in large pieces.

## Popular meats for the barbecue or grill:

| | |
|---|---|
| **Ground meat** | **Pork and beef** (for kabobs) |
| **Sausages** | |
| **Lamb chops** | **Steak** |
| **Lamb** (from the leg for kabobs) | **Chicken pieces** |
| | **Spareribs** |

## Versatile meats for quickly prepared dishes:

| | |
|---|---|
| **Side bacon** | **Ground beef** |
| **Chicken** | **Ham** |
| Peameal bacon | Salami |
| Pepperoni | |

## Meats for one pot meals and stews:

| | |
|---|---|
| **Chicken** | **Pork** |
| **Lamb** | **Garlic sausage** |
| **Beef** | |

## FROM THE DAIRY CASE

| | |
|---|---|
| **Large eggs** | **Mozzarella cheese** |
| **Milk** | **Cream cheese** |
| **Cheddar cheese** | Mayonnaise |
| **Parmesan cheese** | Shortening |
| **Butter** | Lard |
| **Whipping cream** | Cottage cheese |
| **Table cream** | Yogurt |
| **Sour cream** | Buttermilk |
| **Swiss cheese** | Feta cheese |

## FROM THE GREEN GROCER

| | |
|---|---|
| Onions | Apples |
| Garlic | Potatoes |
| Tomatoes | Green peppers |
| Green onions | Mushrooms |
| Salad greens | Carrots |
| Parsley | Cucumber |
| Lemons | Limes |
| Celery | And seasonal |
| Ginger root | fruits and |
| Hot peppers | vegetables. |
| Oranges | |

## FROM THE BAKERY
European-style bread
Wholewheat bread
English muffins
Rolls

# Non-Perishables

## CANNED
**Tomatoes** (28 oz/796 mL)
**Tomato paste** (5½ oz/156 mL)
**Baby clams** (5 oz/142 g)
**Crab meat** (6 oz/170 g)
**Anchovy fillets** (2 oz/50 g)
**Olives** (ripe and/or green)
**Mushrooms** (10 oz/284 mL)
**Hot green chillies**
**Sliced pineapple** (14 oz/398 mL)
**Mandarin oranges** (10 oz/284 mL)
**Peach halves** (14 oz/398 mL)
Shrimp (4 oz can/113 g)
Salmon (7¾ oz can/220 g)
Smoked oysters (3.67 oz can/104 g)
Tuna (6½ oz can/185 g)
Lobster (6 oz can/170 g)
Kidney beans (19 oz can/540 mL)
Chick peas (19 oz can/540 mL)
Creamed corn (10 oz can/284 mL)
Kernel corn (12 oz can/341 mL)
Water chestnuts (10 oz can/284 mL)
Vegetable cocktail (48 oz can/1.36 L)

Clamato juice (10 oz can/284 mL)
Artichoke hearts (14 oz can/398 mL)
White asparagus (14 oz can/398 mL)

## PACKAGED

**Flour** (all-purpose)  **Cocoa**
**White sugar**  **Rolled oats**
**Brown sugar**  **Honey**
**Oil**  **Gelatine**
**Vinegar**  **Cornstarch**
**Coffee**  **Almonds**
**Tea**
**Bouillon Cubes** (chicken and beef)
**Rice** (white and/or brown)
**Pasta** (spaghetti or linguine, fettucine or
  egg noodles, rigatoni or tortiglioni)
Granola ingredients (bran flakes, wheat
  germ, non-instant skim milk powder,
  sesame seeds, sunflower seeds, raisins)
Peanuts  Lentils
Peanut Butter  Split peas
Maple syrup  Dried beans
Taco shells  red and white
Corn chips  Dried fruit

## Spice Rack

Salt  Nutmeg
Peppercorns  Ketchup
Dijon-style  Dry Mustard
  mustard  Worcestershire
Thyme  sauce
Bayleaf  Tabasco sauce
Oregano  Soy sauce
Paprika  Basil
Curry powder  Chili powder
Cinnamon  Cumin
Horseradish  Cayenne
Capers  Turmeric
Sweet relish  Mustard seed
Marjoram  Cardamon
Tarragon  Ginger
Celery seed  Cloves
Rosemary  Allspice
Hot pepper flakes  Caraway seed

## The Cook's Cellar

**Dry red wine**  **Beer**
**Dry white wine**  Madeira
**Orange-flavoured**  Rum
  **liqueur**  Brandy

## Loafing Around

The baker's storecupboard.

| | |
|---|---|
| **Baking powder** | **Cornmeal** |
| **Yeast** | **Baking soda** |
| **Vanilla** | **Walnuts** |
| **Icing sugar** | Molasses |
| Unsweetened des- | Unsweetened |
| sicated coconut | and semi-sweet |
| Chocolate chips | chocolate |
| Self-raising flour | |

## Useful Shortcuts

Versatile convenience foods to use when time is short.

| | |
|---|---|
| **Tomato sauce** | **Pancake mix** |
| (7½ oz can/213 mL) | **Pastry mix** |
| **Breadcrumbs** | **Condensed milk** |
| **Biscuit mix** | (14 oz can/300 mL) |
| Chocolate wafers | Barbecue sauce |
| Graham crackers | Freezer bread |
| Lemon pound | dough |
| cake mix | Cream of potato |
| Consommé | soup |
| (10 oz can/284 mL) | (10 oz can/284 mL) |

## The Drinking Man's Checklist

We suggest that you turn to the section 'Thirst Quenchers' to check up on ingredients for special drinks. However, as basics in this department we suggest you have the following on hand.

| | |
|---|---|
| **Ice** | **Unsweetened** |
| **Soda water** | **fruit juices** |
| **Lemons** | **Mint** |
| **Limes** | |

Winter brews benefit from whole spices such as cinnamon sticks, whole cloves and nutmeg, and warm spirits including dark rum, whiskey and brandy.

# In A Pinch—Substitutions

| For | | Substitute |
|---|---|---|
| 1 square (1oz/28g) unsweetened baking chocolate | — | 3 tbsp (50 mL) cocoa plus 1 tbsp (15mL) butter. |
| 1 cup (250 mL) self-raising flour | — | 1 cup minus 2 tbsp (250 mL minus 30 mL) all purpose flour plus a generous teaspoon (7 mL) baking powder and a pinch of salt. |
| 1 cup (250 mL) sour milk or buttermilk | — | 1 tbsp (15 mL) lemon juice or vinegar and milk to make 1 cup (250 mL). Let stand at room temperature for 5 minutes. |
| 1 clove garlic | — | ¼ tsp (1mL) garlic powder |
| 1 small onion | — | 1 tbsp (15mL) dried onion flakes |
| 1 cup (250 mL) honey | — | 1¼ cups (300 mL) sugar plus ¼ cup (50 mL) extra liquid. |
| 1 cup (250 mL) sour cream | — | ¾ cup (175 mL) sour milk plus ⅓ cup (75 mL) butter. |
| 1 cup (250 mL) whipping cream | — | ¾ cup (175 mL) milk and increase butter by ¼-⅓ cup (50 mL-75 mL). |

# Good Food To Wake Up To

**M**ornings are magic on holiday. Instead of the frantic workday dash, there is *time*. Time to arise and enjoy a spectacular sunrise or the wonderful eerie sight of heavy mist slowly lifting off limpid water. Time to drift back to sleep if rain is pattering on the windows. Time to savour freshly brewed coffee and perhaps even whip up a batch of cottage cheese pancakes.

On holiday, mornings don't have to be organized. Everyone goes at his own pace. The early morning fisherman may set off with a slice of last night's pizza in hand. The young ones usually dive into the cereal and toast with peanut butter no matter what good things are offered.

There are times, however, whether it's a long, leisurely breakfast with friends on a sunny deck or a hearty meal before a day on the slopes, when you want to sit down to a real spread.

# Baked Eggs, Spanish Style

*Breakfast is like love: conversation impedes and spectators ruin it.*
*Nicholas Monsarrat*

This recipe serves four but can easily be adapted for one or a crowd. There's a bit of preparation time but no panic time. There's no need to fry, flip, stir, toast and pour juice all at the same moment. The eggs bake quietly in a light tomato sauce, which can be prepared ahead and reheated anytime.

| | | |
|---|---|---|
| 1 tbsp | butter | 15 mL |
| 1 tbsp | oil | 15 mL |
| 1 | garlic clove, minced | 1 |
| 1 | onion, finely chopped | 1 |
| 1 | green pepper, seeded and chopped | 1 |
| 2 | ham slices (optional), chopped | 2 |
| 4 | tomatoes, chopped | 4 |
| 1 tbsp | parsley, chopped | 15 mL |
| | salt and freshly ground pepper | |
| 4 | eggs | 4 |

**\*symbol indicates that the recipe may be prepared ahead up until this point.**

**Set oven** to 400°F (200°C).

**Heat butter** and oil in a heavy frying pan over medium heat. Sauté garlic and onion briefly. Toss in green pepper and cook over medium heat until the vegetables are soft.

**Add ham**, tomatoes and parsley and continue cooking until the sauce is thick and rich. Season with salt and pepper.\*

**Ladle** the sauce into a large shallow baking dish, well oiled, and break the eggs on top in a circular pattern.

**Cover and bake** until the whites of the eggs are set but the yolks are still soft, about 15 minutes.

**Serve** piping hot with crusty rolls, and spicy Bloody Marys.

**Serves 4**

This dish may also be cooked on top of the stove in a large covered frying pan. It becomes quite spectacular if you add a garnish of sliced artichoke hearts, white asparagus and strips of pimiento, all of which you may have on hand in the storecupboard for special occasions.

# Frittata

This giant, savoury omelette will satisfy a group. Serve it sizzling from the skillet.

| | | |
|---|---|---|
| ¼ cup | butter | 50 mL |
| 1 | onion, chopped | 1 |
| ¼ lb | mushrooms, sliced | 125 g |
| 1-10 oz bag | spinach, cooked, drained and chopped | 1-284 g bag |
| ½ cup | chopped ham | 125 mL |
| | grated nutmeg | |
| | salt and freshly ground pepper | |
| 8 | eggs, beaten | 8 |
| 1 tbsp | grated Parmesan cheese | 15 mL |

**Set oven** to 350°F (180°C).

**Heat butter** in a 12" (29 cm) skillet with an ovenproof handle. Add the onion, mushrooms, spinach and ham. Heat through to distribute the flavours. Season to taste with a little nutmeg, salt and pepper.*

**When ready** to serve, return the skillet to the heat and when the spinach mixture is hot, pour in the beaten eggs. Cook until the bottom has set (approximately 3 minutes).

**Sprinkle** with Parmesan cheese and place in the oven. Cook 2-3 minutes, until slightly puffed and golden.

**Serve with** sliced tomatoes and crispy French bread.

**Serves 4 to 6**

The only trick here is not to overcook the eggs. (The centre should be moist.) If you do, may we suggest you serve it cold as egg pie! For variety use bacon or back bacon instead of ham or add a chopped tomato or a sliced zucchini; the selection of flavouring ingredients is not written in stone. Try combining the eggs with some leftover Ratatouille Niçoise (page 102).

# Eggs Baked in Tomatoes

So simple and yet so good.

| 4 | tomatoes | 4 |
|---|---|---|
| ¼ cup | melted butter | 50 mL |
| 4 | eggs | 4 |
| 1 tbsp | chopped parsley | 15 mL |
| | salt and freshly ground pepper | |
| 2 | English muffins, cut in half, toasted and buttered | 2 |

**Set oven** to 350°F (180°C).

**Slice across** the stem ends of the tomatoes, scoop out the insides and set upside down to drain off the juices.

**Brush** the outsides of the tomatoes with butter and set them snugly in a small buttered baking dish. Lightly season the insides of the tomatoes with salt and pepper and spoon a little butter into each cavity.*

**Break an egg** into each tomato, sprinkle with parsley and drizzle remaining butter on top.*

**Bake** until the eggs are just set, about 15-20 minutes.

**Serve on** toasted English muffins.

**Serves 2 or 4**

## Breakfast Peppers

Take 3 or 4 hot banana peppers, remove the stem ends, slice in two and, if you don't want to lose your cool, remove the seeds. (See cautionary note on hot peppers, page 84.) Heat a little oil in a pan, toss in the peppers, cover and cook over low heat to soften. Serve with eggs for breakfast, barbecued lamb chops for dinner or as a snack any time.

# Sweet Soufflé Omelette

This may sound as though it should be served in a fancy restaurant, but it takes little effort to prepare.

| | | |
|---|---|---|
| 4 | eggs, separated | 4 |
| 1 tbsp | table cream | 15 mL |
| 1 tsp | sugar | 5 mL |
| 1 tsp | grated lemon rind | 5 mL |
| 1 tbsp | butter | 15 mL |
| | jam or fresh fruit preserve | |

**Set oven** to broil.

**Beat egg yolks** with the cream and sugar until thoroughly combined and stir in the lemon rind.

**Whisk egg whites** until stiff. Fold into the egg yolk mixture.

**Heat butter** in a skillet with an ovenproof handle until it sizzles. Pour in the egg mixture and cook over medium-low heat about 2-3 minutes.

**Sprinkle** with a little sugar and place under the broiler until golden brown. Spread with jam or fresh fruit preserve and serve immediately, straight from the pan.

**Serves 4**

A chilled fruity white wine makes this an elegant brunch.

# Savoury Soufflé Omelette

| | | |
|---|---|---|
| 4 | eggs, separated | 4 |
| 1 tbsp | table cream | 15 mL |
| 2 tbsp | grated Swiss cheese | 25 mL |
| 1 tsp | chopped parsley | 5 mL |
| 1 tsp | chopped chives | 5 mL |
| | salt and freshly ground pepper | |
| 1 tbsp | butter | 15 mL |
| 1 tbsp | grated Parmesan cheese | 15 mL |

**Set oven** to broil.

**Beat egg yolks** into the cream and stir in Swiss cheese, herbs, salt and pepper.

**Whisk egg whites** until stiff. Fold into the yolk mixture.

**Heat butter** in a skillet with an ovenproof handle until it sizzles. Pour in the egg mixture and cook over medium-heat about 2-3 minutes.

**Sprinkle** the top of the omelette with a little grated Parmesan cheese before slipping under the broiler. Broil until lightly browned.

**Serve** from the pan.

**Serves 4**

# Eggs Benedict

| 2 | English muffins, cut in half | 2 |
|---|---|---|
| | butter | |
| 4 | back bacon or ham slices | 4 |
| 4 | tomato slices | 4 |
| 4 | eggs, poached | 4 |
| | Nippy Cheese Sauce or Holiday Hollandaise (page 30) | |

**Toast and butter** the English muffins.

**Sauté** the back bacon or ham in a little butter. Place a slice on each muffin half.

**Top with** a tomato slice and a poached egg.

**Pour** cheese sauce or hollandaise over top.

**Sprinkle with** paprika and finely chopped parsley, if you wish.

**Serve with** Bloody Marys (page 206).

**Serves 2 or 4**

**How to Poach an Egg:** We know—in an egg poacher. But it's just as easy in a frying pan. What you do need is fresh eggs. Old eggs have a runny white and you'll end up with something that looks more like an explosion. Fill a frying pan with water and add 1 teaspoon (5 mL) vinegar. The vinegar helps to set the whites. You'll need enough water to cover the eggs (about 2"/5 cm). Bring to a simmer. (This means the water will have lots of tiny bubbles in it but no giant ones.) Break the eggs, one by one, into a cup and slide into the water, one at a time. Cover and cook until the yolks are coated with a light film and the whites are set. Remove with a slotted spoon.

# Nippy Cheese Sauce

# Holiday Hollandaise

Delicious on poached eggs, or steamed cauliflower, or broccoli. Spoon over fish or chicken and bake in the oven.

| 2 tbsp | butter | 25 mL |
|---|---|---|
| 3 tbsp | flour | 45 mL |
| 1½ cups | milk | 375 mL |
| 1 cup | grated Cheddar or Swiss cheese | 250 mL |
| | salt and freshly ground pepper | |
| | dash each Tabasco and Worcestershire sauce | |

**Melt butter** in a small saucepan. Blend in flour and cook briefly over medium heat.

**Lift pan** from heat and whisk in milk. Cook and stir over medium heat until nicely thickened. Stir in grated cheese and whisk until melted. Season to taste.

**Makes 2 cups (500 mL)**

Unless you're an old hand at making hollandaise in a frying pan or pot, we recommend this blender version. If you don't have a blender, make a cheese sauce instead.

| 3 | egg yolks | 3 |
|---|---|---|
| 2 tbsp | lemon juice (juice of ½ lemon) | 25 mL |
| ½ tsp | dry mustard | 2 mL |
| ½ tsp | salt | 2 mL |
| ½ cup | melted butter | 125 mL |

**Place egg yolks**, lemon juice and seasonings in a blender jar.

**Melt butter** in a small pot. Blend egg yolks 1 minute.

**Add the butter** gradually to the egg yolks, blending constantly.

**Makes 1 cup (250 mL)**

# Eggs Florentine

Eggs and spinach are wonderful together. Poached eggs are particularly good nestled in a bed of spinach and laden with hollandaise. If that frightens you, use fried eggs instead and a creamy cheese sauce.

| 4 | eggs, poached | 4 |
|---|---|---|
| 1 | onion, chopped | 1 |
| 1 tbsp | butter | 15 mL |
| 1-10 oz bag | spinach, cooked, drained and chopped | 1-284 g |
| | salt and freshly ground pepper | |
| | nutmeg | |
| | Nippy Cheese Sauce or Holiday Hollandaise | |

**While eggs** are poaching, cook the onion in butter over medium heat. Toss in the spinach. Season with a pinch of salt, pepper and grated nutmeg.

**Place** a few spoonfuls on each plate. Top with a poached egg and smother in sauce.

**For colour**, sprinkle with paprika and serve with a few tomato slices.

**Serves 2 or 4**

**Tip:** Poached eggs may be made in advance and kept in cold water until ready to use. When ready to serve, simply slide into a pan of simmering water and heat 15 seconds.

# Creamed Eggs with Crab

This is terrific company fare for breakfast or brunch.

| | | |
|---|---|---|
| 2 tbsp | butter | 30 mL |
| 2 | green onions, finely chopped | 2 |
| 1-6 oz | can snow crabmeat | 1-170 g |
| ½ cup | table cream | 125 mL |
| 6 | eggs | 6 |
| | pinch cayenne | |
| | salt and pepper to taste | |
| | sprig of finely chopped parsley | |

**Melt butter** in a heavy frying pan. Add onion and sauté briefly. Stir in the crab and cream and cook gently until mixture is heated through.

**Beat eggs** with the cayenne, salt and pepper, and add to the crab. Stir and cook over low heat until eggs are set.

**Remove** from heat. Sprinkle with parsley and serve on toast.

**Serves 4**

This is also good with salmon or lobster. Season the crab mixture with a pinch of tarragon.

# Superb Scrambled Eggs

Brief attentive stirring over gentle heat and prompt action as the eggs begin to thicken—these are the critical factors in making superb scrambled eggs.

| 1 tbsp | butter | 15 mL |
|--------|--------|-------|
| 2-3 | eggs | 2-3 |
| | salt | |
| | dash Tabasco | |
| 1 tbsp | table cream | 15 mL |
| | freshly ground pepper | |

**Melt butter** in a good, heavy pan (preferably one with a non-stick interior, to make clean-up easier) over medium-low heat.

**Blend eggs** in a small bowl with a pinch of salt and a dash of Tabasco and pour into pan.

**Gently stir** eggs as they thicken. When eggs are almost set, lift pan from heat and stir in cream. (Eggs will continue to cook from the heat of the pan.) Season with salt and freshly ground pepper.

**Serve with** grilled side bacon and sausages, or with thick slices of pea-meal back bacon fried in butter, and crisp toasted wholewheat bread or hot cornmeal muffins.

**Serves 1**

On special mornings first sauté sliced mushrooms in a little butter with chopped green onion and a pinch of tarragon. Add to the pan just as the eggs begin to thicken.

For extra creamy scrambled eggs with a pleasant tang, replace the cream with 2 tablespoons (25 mL) soft cream cheese and add chopped chives or parsley. Try adding a few slivers of smoked salmon; it's wonderful!

**Chives substitution:** If a recipe calls for chives and you don't have any, use the green tops of green onions.

# Pepperoni Spoon Bread

A tasty dish for brunch when served with a crisp green salad and sliced tomatoes. The texture falls somewhere between that of bread and a soufflé.

| | | |
|---|---|---|
| 2 cups | milk | 500 mL |
| 1 cup | yellow cornmeal | 250 mL |
| 2 tbsp | butter | 25 mL |
| 1½ cups | grated Cheddar cheese | 375 mL |
| 4 | eggs, separated | 4 |
| 2 | carrots, grated | 2 |
| 1 cup | thinly sliced pepperoni | 250 mL |

**Set oven** to 350°F (180°C).

**Combine** milk and cornmeal in a saucepan. Cook and stir over low heat 5 minutes. The mixture will thicken slightly.

**Remove** from heat and whisk in butter and cheese.

**In a large bowl**, beat egg yolks until creamy. First mix a little of the hot cornmeal mixture into the egg yolks, then blend in the rest of the cornmeal, the grated carrot and pepperoni.

**Beat** egg whites until stiff and fold into cornmeal.

**Spoon into** an 8" x 8" (2 L) baking dish and bake about 40 minutes, until golden brown and firm to the touch.

**Serves 6**

# Bacon and Onion Tart

Tasty and versatile, this tart also travels well.

| 1-9" | partially baked pie shell (see page 182) | 1-23 cm |
|------|------------------------------------------|---------|
| 4 | bacon or ham slices | 4 |
| 2 tbsp | butter | 25 mL |
| 4 | medium onions, sliced | 4 |
| 4 | eggs | 4 |
| 1 cup | table cream | 250 mL |
| | salt and freshly ground pepper | |
| | pinch ground nutmeg | |

**Set oven** to 325°F (160°C).

**Lightly brown** the bacon, cut into thin slices and arrange in pastry shell.

**Melt butter** in a large pan, toss in onions and cook gently over medium heat until soft. Spoon on top of bacon.

**Whisk** together remaining ingredients and pour into pie shell. Dot top with a little extra butter.

**Bake** 30-40 minutes, until filling is set.

**Serves 6**

# Basic Pancakes—Canadian, Eh?

A holiday breakfast mainstay—especially for trencherman teenage appetites.

| | | |
|---|---|---|
| 2 cups | flour | 500 mL |
| 2 tbsp | sugar | 25 mL |
| 2 tsp | baking powder | 10 mL |
| | pinch salt | |
| 2 | eggs | 2 |
| 2-2½ cups | milk | 500-625 mL |
| 2 tbsp | melted butter or oil | 25 mL |

**Toss** the dry ingredients together in a large bowl.

**Beat eggs** lightly and combine with milk.

**Swiftly stir** the liquid into the dry ingredients and add melted butter or oil.

**Set griddle** or frying pan over medium-high heat. Grease lightly if the pan does not have a non-stick surface. When the pan is nice and hot but not smoking, add the pancake batter—an almost-full ¼-cup (50 mL) measure makes a good-sized pancake.

**When** the tops of the pancakes begin to form a smooth skin with small bubbles on the surface, turn the pancakes over and brown on the other side.

**Serve hot** with lashings of butter and maple syrup and broiled bacon and sausages.

**Makes 12 pancakes**

**Apple-Cinnamon Pancakes:** Stir 1 teaspoon (5 mL) ground cinnamon into the dry ingredients and quickly add 1 cup (250 mL) grated apple to the batter with the melted butter.

**Blueberry Pancakes:** Add 1 cup (250 mL) blueberries to the batter with the melted butter.

**Buttermilk Pancakes:** Buttermilk makes pancakes with an exceptionally light texture. Simply replace the baking powder with 1 teaspoon (5 mL) baking soda and use buttermilk instead of fresh milk.

# Maple Syrup Glazed Sausages

A hint of maple flavour and a delicate sweetness make even a dull sausage something special.

| 3 tbsp | butter | 45 mL |
|---|---|---|
| 2 | onions, thinly sliced | 2 |
| 4 | apples, peeled, cored and sliced | 4 |
| 1 lb | sausages | 500 g |
| ¼ cup | maple syrup | 50 mL |

**Set oven** to 350°F (180°C)

**Sauté onion** and apple in butter in a large frying pan until lightly browned. Remove to a shallow baking dish.

**In the same pan** brown the sausages well on all sides. Lay them on top of the onions and apples and pour maple syrup over the top.

**Bake** about 30 minutes.

**Serves 4**

Wonderful served with hot corn bread.

## Home Fries

Boil potatoes (1 per person) until tender. Peel and slice. Melt butter in frying pan over medium heat. Toss in potatoes and some chopped onion (or green onions or chives). Sprinkle with paprika. Cook, turning frequently, until nicely browned on both sides. Salt and pepper to taste. Scrumptious!

# Country Inn Pancakes

If you like to serve maple syrup with pancakes, warm it first to bring out the pure maple flavour.

| | | |
|---|---|---|
| 6 | eggs | 6 |
| 1 cup | cottage cheese | 250 mL |
| ½ cup | flour | 125 mL |
| 2 tbsp | melted butter | 25 mL |
| | pinch sugar | |
| | pinch salt | |

**Beat eggs** and cheese in a large bowl until smooth. Blend in the flour. Stir in the remaining ingredients.

**Melt** a little extra butter in a large frying pan over medium heat and, when the pan is hot, add the batter, ¼ cup at a time, to form thin pancakes.

**Cook until** the pancakes are lightly brown on the underside, then flip and cook briefly on the other side.

**Serve** these delicate pancakes with sweet butter and homemade preserves, sliced fresh fruit or maple syrup.

**Serves 4**

For a change of taste, fold a pinch of cinnamon and a thinly sliced banana into the batter.

**Tip:** Young people are always hungry for breakfast before the cook is ready to get up. One of our young guests brings along a large stock of his favourite sugar-coated cereal for these emergencies. We suggest you have a supply of serve-yourself cereal on hand and show the under-20s where it's kept!

# A Little Pot o'Jam

Here's a way to make your own jam without feeling as if you're running a factory.

| | | |
|---|---|---|
| 2 cups | fresh berries, sliced | 500 mL |
| 1½ cups | sugar | 375 mL |
| 2 tbsp | lemon juice | 25 mL |

**Press berries** lightly to release some of the juices.

**Pour** into a pot, bring to a boil and cook over medium heat 3-4 minutes.

**Add sugar** (it's best if you warm it in the oven first), and cook until dissolved. Stir in the lemon juice.

**Spoon onto** fresh peaches, ice cream or yogurt for a delicious dessert, or serve with buttery pancakes.

The jam will keep refrigerated for several days. It will drip and run but will taste fresh and wonderful.

**Makes 2 cups (500 mL)**

**Fresh Fruit Preserve:** Our favourite jam is made from fresh strawberries, sliced and mounded on a piece of toast oozing with melted butter. Take a knife and squash the whole mess. It's superb made with raspberries and peaches too.

# Fruit Cup

Any fresh fruit in season makes a light and refreshing breakfast. Try strawberries, raspberries or fresh pineapple.

| 1 | cantaloupe | 1 |
| 1 | honeydew melon | 1 |
| 1 tbsp | sugar | 15 mL |
| 4 | fresh mint sprigs, finely chopped | 4 |
| | juice of 2 limes | |

**Peel and seed** melons. Cut flesh into bite-sized pieces or make melon balls if you have the small scooping tool. Sprinkle fruit with sugar.

**Toss with** fresh mint and lime juice. Chill overnight or serve right away.

**Serve with** a basket of warm cornmeal muffins (page 181).

**Serves 4**

# Comfort Food

When you wake up in the morning with a chilled nose and you look outside at mountainous drifts of snow, there is nothing as comforting as a steaming bowl of porridge.

| 2 cups | milk | 500 mL |
| ¾ cup | quick-cooking rolled oats | 175 mL |
| | pinch salt | |

**Heat milk** in a medium-sized pot. Stir in rolled oats and salt.

**Cook and stir** 5 minutes over low heat. Remove from heat, cover and let stand 5 minutes.

**Serve with** additional milk or cream and brown sugar or honey. If you like, add a sprinkling of granola or raisins.

**Serves 4**

# Granola

A great wholesome breakfast cereal and snack: good with yogurt and fruit.

| | | |
|---|---|---|
| 1 cup | sesame seeds | 250 mL |
| 1 cup | sunflower seeds | 250 mL |
| 5 cups | rolled oats | 1.25 L |
| 1 cup | bran flakes | 250 mL |
| 1 cup | wheat germ | 250 mL |
| 1 cup | non-instant dry milk powder | 250 mL |
| 1 cup | sliced almonds | 250 mL |
| 1 cup | raisins | 250 mL |
| ½ cup | vegetable oil | 125 mL |
| 1 cup | honey | 250 mL |
| 1 tbsp | vanilla | 15 mL |
| 1 tsp | salt | 5 mL |

**Set oven** to 250°F (120°C).

**Combine** dry ingredients, except for the raisins, in a large mixing bowl.

**Heat oil** and honey together over gentle heat. (Heating makes mixture more liquid and easier to mix.)

**Add vanilla** and salt and pour over dry mix.

**Get in** there with your fingers and thoroughly combine ingredients.

**Spread** mixture on two shallow baking trays and bake about 45 minutes, turning the mixture over occasionally so that it toasts evenly.

**Stir in** raisins and cool completely before storing in large jars.

**Makes 12 cups (3 L)**

**Tip:** Toast the sunflower and sesame seeds 10 minutes first and grind or crush them. They are then more readily digested. Add the ground seeds to the toasted oats with the raisins. Don't toast the raisins; they burn easily and get tough.

# The Happy Hour

The happy hour may begin at noon and has been known to last all day. It can be one of those times when a crowd of thirsty and hungry people just happens by, or it may be a formal invitation for cocktails down the lake at six, when you have to put on your shoes and comb your hair. This is the time when we reminisce about the good times of other years. When we hear the latest on old Pops, who has sunk his boat so often by leaving the bailer open that he now puts a tin can on his foot each time he pulls the plug, as a reminder to put it back; Peter, who ran out of gas for the fourth time and, for the fourth time, didn't have a paddle with him; John and his fish stories about the killer muskie that got away, today and yesterday and the day before....

Happy hour food has to suit many different situations. Sometimes you need a small bite to fill the gap before dinner; at other times the food must be more substantial for those who skipped lunch. Sometimes there is time to plan ahead, but most often you turn to the store cupboard for last-minute inspiration.

# Spicy Clam Dip

# Cucumber Dip

Part of the secret of success in life is to eat what you like and let the food fight it out inside.

*Mark Twain*

Kids love it—as long as you don't tell them it has clams in it.

| 1-5 oz | can clams | 1-142 g |
|---|---|---|
| ½ lb | cream cheese | 250 g |
| 2 tbsp | lemon juice | 25 mL |
| 2 | green onions, finely chopped | 2 |
| 2 tsp | grated horseradish | 10 mL |
| | salt and pepper | |

**Drain** clams, saving liquid, and mince.

**Blend lemon** juice and clam liquid with cream cheese until creamy and smooth. Stir in onions, horseradish and minced clams and season with salt and pepper to taste. Cover and chill a few hours.

**Serve with** crisp, raw vegetables.

**Makes about 2 cups (500 mL)**

Not only serves as a refreshing dip for a snack, but as a soothing side dish to spicy barbecued or curried meats.

| 1 | cucumber | 1 |
|---|---|---|
| 2 | garlic cloves, crushed | 2 |
| | salt and freshly ground pepper | |
| 2 tbsp | oil | 25 mL |
| 1 tbsp | vinegar | 15 mL |
| 2 cups | Balkan-style plain yogurt | 500 mL |

**Peel**, seed and grate cucumber.

**Combine** garlic, salt, pepper, oil and vinegar. Stir into yogurt. Drain excess moisture from cucumber and fold into yogurt.

**Serve with** fresh vegetable strips.

**Makes about 2 cups (500 mL)**

# Chili con Queso

This is a hearty, spicy cheese dip served warmed. Use leftovers to make delicious Tex-Mex Nachos.

| | | |
|---|---|---|
| 1 tbsp | oil | 15 mL |
| 1 | onion, finely chopped | 1 |
| 1 | garlic clove, minced | 1 |
| 1-14 oz | can tomatoes | 1-398 mL |
| 1 tsp | hot pepper flakes | 5 mL |
| 1¼ lb | Cheddar cheese, grated | 625 g |
| 2 tbsp | flour | 25 mL |

**Cook onion** and garlic in oil over medium-high until tender in a large saucepan. Drain tomatoes, reserving juice, and roughly chop. Add tomatoes, juice and hot pepper flakes to onion mixture. Cook the whole lot about 15 minutes.*

**Toss cheese** with flour and gradually add to tomato sauce. Cook and stir over low heat until well blended.

**Spoon into** a chafing dish or crockery pot and serve with a bowl of corn or tortilla chips.

### Feeds a roomful

You may use fresh or canned green chilies (1 tablespoon/15 mL minced) instead of hot pepper flakes.

**To finely mince garlic without a garlic press:** Hold a fork vertically on a plate, tines down. Rub the garlic clove across the back of the fork at the end of the tines.

## Dip It

One of our favourite vegetable dips sounds ho-hum! However, it's superb. Simply combine 1 package vegetable soup mix without noodles with 2 cups (500 mL) sour cream. Refrigerate covered overnight.* Excellent texture, colour and flavour.

# Zucchini Fritters

These take work, but are they worth it!

| | | |
|---|---|---|
| 4 | zucchini | 4 |
| ½ cup | flour | 125 mL |
| 2 | eggs, beaten | 2 |
| 1 cup | breadcrumbs | 250 mL |
| ½ tsp | salt | 2 mL |
| ¼ tsp | freshly ground pepper | 1 mL |
| | oil for deep frying | |
| 1 | lemon | 1 |

**Slice zucchini** lengthwise in strips, (½"/ 1.5 cm pieces) usually in eighths. If very long, cut in half. Dip in flour, then beaten egg and seasoned breadcrumbs. Coat zucchini well.

**Deep fry** until crisp and golden. Squirt with lemon juice. Devour!

**Serves 4**

**Fritter Potpourri:** Prepare mushrooms, cauliflower, cubes of mozarella and Cheddar cheese in the same way as zucchini fritters. Absolutely superb!

# Nippy Cheese Bites

An old-time favourite. It's fun to make a variety of cheese bites: sprinkle some with sesame seeds and add a pinch of dried herbs (basil or oregano) to others.

| | | |
|---|---|---|
| ½ cup | butter | 125 mL |
| ½ lb | Cheddar cheese, grated (about 2 cups/ 500 mL) | 250 g |
| 1 cup | flour | 250 mL |
| | pinch salt | |
| ½ tsp | Tabasco | 2 mL |

**Set oven** to 400°F (200°C).

**Cream** together butter and grated cheese and blend in remaining ingredients.

**Set teaspoonfuls** of dough on a cookie sheet and flatten with the tines of a fork.

**Bake** 10-15 minutes, until golden and crisp.

**Makes about 24**

These may be prepared in advance, frozen on cookie sheets and stored in the freezer in a plastic bag. Bake as needed.

**Olive-Stuffed Cheese Bites:** Flatten small balls of dough in the palm of the hand and wrap around stuffed olives.*

# Salmon Mousse

Make this mousse in a loaf pan or a mould. It freezes well or may be kept refrigerated for two to three days. Great with crackers or thin slices of dark bread. Serve with sour cream mixed with freshly chopped dill.

| | | |
|---|---|---|
| 1-1 lb | can red salmon | 1-500 g |
| 2 tbsp | unflavoured gelatine | 25 mL |
| 1 cup | chicken stock | 250 mL |
| 1 tsp | Worcestershire sauce | 5 mL |
| 1 | small onion, finely chopped | 1 |
| 1 cup | mayonnaise | 250 mL |
| | juice of 1 lemon | |
| | dash Tabasco | |
| 1 tbsp | chopped fresh dill | 15 mL |
| | salt and freshly ground pepper to taste | |

**Drain salmon** and pick out skin and bones.

**In a small bowl**, soften gelatine in ¼ cup (50 mL) of the chicken stock and place over a pan of hot water. Stir until completely dissolved, then set aside until almost cool.

**Blend** or whip together all ingredients until smooth. Pour into a lightly oiled loaf pan. Cover and chill until set.

**Serve**, unmolded, on a plate lined with lettuce leaves and surrounded by whatever fresh vegetable garnish you have, such as tomatoes or cucumbers. It looks very impressive.

**Serves 8**

# Smoked Oyster Pâté

The topping of chopped parsley and walnuts not only makes this easy pâté very good to look at, but it adds freshness and crunch to the tangy spread beneath.

| | | |
|---|---|---|
| 1-3.6 oz | can smoked oysters, drained | 1-104 g |
| 2 | green onions, chopped | 2 |
| ½ cup | cream cheese | 125 mL |
| ¼ cup | sour cream | 50 mL |
| 2 tbsp | lemon juice | 25 mL |
| ½ tsp | salt | 2 mL |
| ½ cup | chopped walnuts | 125 mL |
| ¼ cup | chopped fresh parsley | 50 mL |

**Blend** or mash the smoked oysters. Combine with onions, cream cheese, sour cream, lemon juice and salt.

**Pile** into a bowl and cover with walnuts and parsley. Chill.*

**Serve with** melba toast, crisp fingers of wholewheat toast or pita chips.

**Serves 4**

## Pita Chips

Pita bread is readily available. These chips are easy to make and fun to serve on their own or with a dip.

Brush pita bread with melted butter. Sprinkle with Parmesan cheese, a little garlic salt, celery salt or oregano. Cut into triangles (scissors work well). Place on a baking sheet and bake in a 450°F (230°C) oven until crisp and lightly browned (4-6 minutes).

# Skewered Meat

A neat "loaves and fishes" trick. A small quantity of meat makes a special snack.

| | | |
|---|---|---|
| ½ lb | pork, veal or sirloin steak | 250 g |
| 3 tbsp | oil | 45 mL |
| 2 tbsp | lemon juice | 25 mL |
| 1 | garlic clove, mashed | 1 |
| ½ tsp | dry mustard | 2 mL |
| ½ tsp | Worcestershire sauce | 2 mL |
| 1 | bay leaf | 1 |
| | pinch dried basil | |
| | salt and freshly ground pepper | |

**Cut meat** into bite-sized pieces.

**Combine** remaining ingredients and pour over meat. Marinate several hours.*

**Thread meat** on wooden skewers and grill over charcoal or broil in the oven until nicely browned on all sides.

**Serve with** rounds of fresh bread and the Cucumber Dip (page 44).

**Serves 4 to 6**

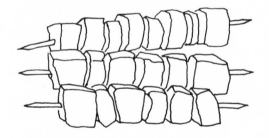

# Clams Casino

A somewhat messy to eat snack, unless you have individual serving dishes. Best to serve at a table and supply each person with a small fork and lots of crusty French-style bread. Of course, use fresh shellfish if you have them.

| | | |
|---|---|---|
| ½ cup | soft butter | 125 mL |
| 2 | green onions, finely chopped | 2 |
| 1 | garlic clove, minced | 1 |
| 1 tbsp | chopped fresh parsley | 15 mL |
| ¼ tsp | dried basil | 1 mL |
| ¼ tsp | salt | 1 mL |
| | pinch freshly ground pepper | |

| | | |
|---|---|---|
| ½ cup | breadcrumbs | 125 mL |
| ¼ cup | grated Parmesan cheese | 50 mL |
| 2-5 oz | cans baby clams or oysters | 2-142 g |
| 4 | bacon slices, cut in small strips | 4 |

**Set oven** to 400°F (200°C).

**Combine** butter, onions, garlic, parsley, basil, salt and pepper. Mix breadcrumbs with the cheese.

**Drain** clams. Place clams in a buttered shallow baking dish (or individual shells). Spread the herb butter on top and sprinkle with the breadcrumbs and cheese mixture and bacon pieces.*

**Bake** about 10 minutes, then slip briefly under the broiler for the topping to become golden and crispy.

**Serves 6**

51

# Tex-Mex Nachos

Communal snacking food.

| | plain corn chips or tortilla chips | |
| --- | --- | --- |
| 2 cups | grated Cheddar cheese | 500 mL |
| 1 | medium onion, chopped | 1 |
| 2 | tomatoes, chopped | 2 |
| ¼ cup | black or stuffed olives, pitted and chopped | 50 mL |
| 2 | hot peppers, finely chopped (optional) | 2 |
| | sour cream | |

**Set oven** to 350°F (180°C).

**Spread chips** in a single layer, slightly overlapping, on a glass pie plate or shallow baking tray.

**Sprinkle with** Cheddar cheese, onion, tomatoes, olives and hot peppers.

**Bake** about 15 minutes, until nachos are hot and cheese is melted and bubbling.

**Serve with** soothing sour cream and frosty glasses of chilled beer.

### Serves 4 to 8

**Super Nachos:** Spread tortilla chips with a layer of Tex-Mex Meat Filling (page 85); drizzle with Basic Hot Sauce (page 85) and proceed as for Tex-Mex Nachos.

# The Breadbasket

More than just bread. Great munchies for those times when the charcoal seems to be taking forever to get hot.

**Herb-Garlic Bread:** Cut European-style white bread into ½" (1.5 cm) slices, leaving the pieces attached at the bottom. Spread each slice generously with Herb-Garlic Butter (page133). Wrap securely in foil.* Heat in a 400°F (200°C) oven about 15 minutes when needed.

To make a substantial snack or light lunch, tuck a slice of cooked ham and mozzarella cheese between each cut. Wrap securely in foil.* Heat as above. The prepared loaf may be stored in the freezer. Allow about 30 minutes in a hot oven before serving.

**Crisp Garlic Bread:** Cut European-style white bread into generous ½" (1.5 cm) slices. Spread with Herb-Garlic Butter and sprinkle with grated Parmesan cheese. Arrange on a baking sheet and heat in a 400°F (200°C) oven about 10 minutes.

**Italian Cheese Bread:** Cut a French stick into ½" (1.5 cm) slices. Toss together a little chopped fresh tomato, a minced garlic clove, olive oil, oregano and salt. Toast French bread and rub with a cut garlic clove. Spoon tomato mixture onto bread slices and sprinkle with Parmesan cheese. The same mixture is delicious sprinkled with grated mozzarella cheese and then set under the broiler until just melted.

# Garlicky Mushrooms

A tasty hot hors d'oeuvre feast.

| 1 lb | mushrooms | 500 g |
|---|---|---|
| 2 tbsp | butter, melted | 30 mL |
| | Herb-Garlic Butter (page 133) | |

**Set oven** to 400°F (200°C).

**Remove stems** from the mushrooms. Wipe clean with a damp cloth. Brush caps with butter and place on a greased baking sheet, stem side up.

**Place** a teaspoon (5 mL) of filling in each mushroom. Cover with plastic wrap and refrigerate until ready to use.*

**To serve**, place in oven and bake 15-20 minutes, until bubbly and hot. Let cool briefly to finger touch.

**Serves 4**

# Bacon Wrapped Water Chestnuts

An old standby that never loses its popularity.

| 1-10 oz | can water chestnuts, drained | 1-284 mL |
|---|---|---|
| ¼ cup | soy sauce | 50 mL |
| | bacon slices | |

**Slice** the water chestnuts in half and soak in soy sauce 1 hour or more.

**Cut bacon** slices in thirds. Wrap one piece of bacon around each water chestnut and secure with a toothpick. Set on a broiling pan.*

**When ready** to serve, slip under the broiler and cook until bacon is crisp (approximately 5 minutes).

**Serves 4**

# Madeira Mushrooms on Toast

A special treat for intimate occasions.

| | | |
|---|---|---|
| 4 | bread slices, crusts removed | 4 |
| 1 tbsp | butter | 15 mL |
| 2 | green onions, finely chopped | 2 |
| ½ lb | mushrooms, wiped and sliced | 250 g |
| ¼ cup | Madeira | 50 mL |
| ½ cup | whipping cream | 125 mL |
| ½ tsp | dried tarragon | 2 mL |
| | salt and freshly ground pepper | |

**Set oven** to 325°F (160°C).

**Butter bread**, cut in half diagonally and toast in oven until crisp, about 10 minutes.

**Meanwhile** melt butter in a small frying pan. Toss in green onions, mushrooms and a little salt and pepper and cook for 4-5 minutes over medium heat.

**Pour in** Madeira, raise the heat to medium-high and stir while liquid boils down to about a tablespoon (15 mL). Whisk in cream and tarragon and continue to boil until the sauce has thickened slightly.

**Taste** to make sure seasoning is just right. Arrange toast on two plates and pour the mushrooms on top.

**Serve** very hot.

**Serves 2**

This Madeira mushroom sauce is also splendid with grilled or roasted meats.

# Zucchini Cocktail Squares

A popular snack in cottage country.

| | | |
|---|---|---|
| 3½ cups | diced zucchini (skins too!) | 875 mL |
| 1 | small onion, finely chopped | 1 |
| ½ cup | grated old Cheddar cheese | 125 mL |
| 1¼ cups | biscuit mix | 300 mL |
| 1 tsp | dried oregano | 5 mL |
| ¼ cup | vegetable oil | 50 mL |
| 3 | eggs, beaten | 3 |
| ½ tsp | salt | 2 mL |

**Set oven** to 325°F (160°C).

**Combine** all the ingredients in a large bowl. Spoon into a well-greased 9" x 13" (3L) pan. Bake 1 hour, until lightly browned and firm to the touch. Cut into squares.

**Makes 24 2-inch/5 cm squares**

# Grandma's Great Curry Hors d'Oeuvre

Grandma was not one for meat and potatoes.

| | | |
|---|---|---|
| 1½ cups | grated Cheddar cheese | 375 mL |
| ½ cup | minced onion | 125 mL |
| 1 cup | black olives, pitted and chopped | 250 mL |
| ½ cup | mayonnaise | 125 mL |
| 1 tsp | curry powder | 5 mL |
| 6 | slices rye bread | 6 |

**Set oven** to broil.

**Mix** together cheese, onion, olives, mayonnaise and curry powder.

**Cut bread** slices in four and spread with cheese mixture.* Broil 3-5 minutes, until cheese melts.

**Makes 24**

# Cocktail Pie

Popular ingredients arranged in layers make an easy to prepare but special appetizer for a crowd.

| | | |
|---|---|---|
| 6 | hard-boiled eggs | 6 |
| 2 tbsp | mayonnaise | 25 mL |
| | salt and freshly ground pepper | |
| 1 | red onion (or 2 green onions), finely chopped | 1 |
| 1 | cucumber, peeled, seeded and chopped | 1 |
| ½ lb | cream cheese | 250 g |
| 1 cup | sour cream | 250 mL |

**Chop** hard-boiled eggs. Toss with mayonnaise and a little salt and pepper.

**Spread mixture** in a pie plate (about 9"/23 cm diameter). Top with a layer of onion and the chopped cucumber.

**Combine** the cream cheese and the sour cream and spread on top. Refrigerate.

**Garnish** at serving time with a sprinkling of fresh chopped herbs, a few chopped olives or, best of all, a few spoonfuls of salmon roe.

**Serve with** crackers or crisp rye or wholewheat toast.

**Serves 6 or more**

**Crisp Bread:** Home-made crisp bread is tastier than most store-bought crackers. Slice good wholewheat, rye or pumpernickel very thin. Bake until crisp, about 15 minutes, in a 250°F (120°C) oven.

# The Back Burner

There's nothing quite as heartwarming as a mug of hot chunky soup when you arrive at the cottage late on a chilly evening. A cup of minestrone is a quick sustaining snack before the long drive back to the city. We include a small selection of soups. A few are of the 'stick to the ribs' variety, great to make ahead and take along, particularly on winter trips. A few are cool and refreshing for those times when you have had too much sun and too much food and you just fancy something light and tasty.

# Eye Opener

... we have diminished the expense, without impoverishing the preparations; and the rational epicure will be as well pleased with them as the rational economist.
*The Cook Not Mad*
*(Canada's first cookbook)*

The perfect beginning for a leisurely summer lunch.

| | | |
|---|---|---|
| 4 oz | vodka | 125 mL |
| 4 cups | can vegetable cocktail, well chilled | 1 L |
| 1-10 oz | can Clamato juice, well chilled | 1-284 mL |
| 2 tbsp | lemon juice | 25 mL |
| | dash Tabasco | |
| | squirt Worcestershire sauce | |
| | salt and freshly ground pepper to taste | |
| | Garnish: sour cream chopped green onion green pepper cucumber tomato | |

**Combine** all ingredients.

**Pour into** glass bowls (glass goblets are fun). Spoon a dollop of sour cream on top and sprinkle with a tablespoon or two (15-25 mL) of chopped vegetables.

**Serves 6**

**Quick and Chilly:** Keep a couple of cans of consommé in the refrigerator. Spoon the jelled consommé into small bowls lined with bibb lettuce. Sprinkle with bits of chopped vegetables: green pepper, carrot, tomato.

# Soup for All Seasons

A creamed vegetable soup, hot or cold, can often serve as a light lunch or supper. A basket of hot crusty rolls makes a perfect complement. Here's a basic recipe.

| | | |
|---|---|---|
| 3 tbsp | butter | 45 mL |
| 1 | onion, finely chopped | 1 |
| 1 cup | finely chopped vegetable—either carrots, spinach (use ½ pound/ 250 g trimmed), celery, mushrooms, broccoli or zucchini | 250 mL |
| 2 cups | chicken stock | 500 mL |
| 1 cup | table cream | 250 mL |
| | salt, freshly ground pepper and nutmeg to taste | |
| | squeeze lemon juice | |

**Melt butter** in a large saucepan. Toss in the onion and cook over medium heat until softened.

**Add vegetable** and cook 2 minutes.

**Stir in** the stock. Bring just to a boil and simmer until the vegetable is tender.

**Stir in** the cream, taste for seasonings and add lemon juice.

**Serve** hot or chilled.

**If you like** a smooth consistency, purée the vegetable and stock mixture after it has cooled. Return to the pot and stir in the cream.

**Serves 4**

# Shellfish Soup

A delicate soup open to all manner of variations. Try replacing cream with Balkan-style yogurt for a very refreshing chilled version.

| | | |
|---|---|---|
| 3 | green onions, chopped | 3 |
| 2 tbsp | butter | 25 mL |
| 2 | medium cucumbers, peeled, seeded and sliced | 2 |
| 1 cup | chicken stock | 250 mL |
| ½ cup | table cream | 125 mL |
| | salt and white pepper | |
| 1-6 oz | can lobster, crabmeat or shrimp | 1-170 g |
| 2 tbsp | lemon juice | 25 mL |
| | chopped fresh chives and dill | |

**In a medium** saucepan, cook onions in butter over medium heat until tender. Add cucumber and stock and simmer, covered, until cucumber is soft. Blend mixture in a food processor or push through a sieve.

**Stir in** cream, salt and pepper.

**Pick over** shellfish to remove stray pieces of shell and cartilage and stir into cream and cucumber mixture.

**Flavour with** lemon juice and fresh herbs.

**Serve** hot or chilled.

**Serves 4**

**Tip:** There is nothing quite as refreshing as a chilled cucumber soup. Simply omit the shellfish.

# Gazpacho

A pleasant, refreshing summer soup. Serve with Crisp Garlic Bread (page 53) for a light meal.

| | | |
|---|---|---|
| 1 | garlic clove, crushed | 1 |
| 1 tsp | salt | 5 mL |
| ½ slice | white bread, crusts removed | |
| 2 tbsp | olive oil | 25 mL |
| 1-28 oz | can tomatoes, drained and finely chopped | 1-796 mL |
| 2 tbsp | vinegar | 25 mL |
| 2 tbsp | onion, chopped | 25 mL |
| 1 | cucumber, peeled seeded and chopped | 1 |
| 1 | green pepper, seeded and chopped | 1 |
| | salt and freshly ground pepper | |

Garnish:
croutons
chopped green onion
sour cream
chopped vegetables
(cucumber, green
pepper and tomato)

**Crush garlic** in a large bowl with the salt. Add bread and oil and let stand 30 minutes.

**Stir** in tomatoes, vinegar, onion and half the cucumber and green pepper. (Save the other half for garnish.) Blend until smooth (this is accomplished quickly and easily in a blender or a food mill). If you wish to thin the soup a little, use ice cubes, ice water or chilled stock. Season with salt and pepper to taste.

**Serve** ice cold in chilled bowls, accompanied with bowls of assorted garnish.

**Serves 4**

# Speedy Clam Chowder

Made with ingredients from the store-cupboard and ready in ten minutes.

| | | |
|---|---|---|
| 1 tbsp | butter | 15 mL |
| 2 | slices bacon, chopped | 2 |
| 1 | small onion, chopped | 1 |
| 1-5 oz | can minced clams | 1-142 g |
| 1-10 oz | can cream of potato soup | 1-284 mL |
| 1 cup | milk | 250 mL |
| 1 cup | table cream | 250 mL |
| | pinch thyme | |
| | salt and freshly ground pepper | |

**In a heavy pot**, sauté bacon and onion in butter until softened.

**Add** clams, soup, milk, cream and thyme. Heat through.

**Season** with salt and pepper to taste.

**Ladle** into deep warm bowls and serve with soda crackers.

**Serves 4**

**Quick and Hot:** Heat a can of consommé. Add a few grated or finely chopped vegetables (carrots, green pepper or celery). Stir in a little sherry or Madeira, and heat through. Serve with toasted Beer Break (page 178).

# Minestrone

This soup takes little effort. Push to the back of the stove and let simmer away while you put your feet up.

| | | |
|---|---|---|
| 3 | slices bacon, cut in strips | 3 |
| 1 | garlic clove, minced | 1 |
| 1 | onion, finely chopped | 1 |
| 1 tbsp | olive oil | 15 mL |
| 3 | tomatoes, peeled, seeded and chopped | 3 |
| 6 cups | beef stock | 1.5 L |
| 1 | carrot, cut in rounds | 1 |
| ½ lb | green beans, chopped | 250 g |
| 1 stalk | celery, chopped | 1 stalk |
| 2 | zucchini, cut in rounds | 2 |
| ½ cup | macaroni or other pasta | 125 mL |
| | salt and freshly ground pepper | |
| | few sprigs parsley or basil | |
| | grated Parmesan cheese | |

**Fry bacon**, garlic and onion in oil in a large heavy pot over medium-high heat. Add tomatoes and cook 5 minutes. Stir in stock and prepared vegetables. Bring to a boil, partially cover the pot and simmer 30 minutes.*

**Add macaroni**, salt, pepper and parsley and cook until pasta is tender about, 10 minutes.

**Serve** piping hot with plenty of grated Parmesan cheese.

**Serves 6 to 8**

# Mulligatawny

Mulligatawny refers to a group of Indian soups, the name meaning 'pepper water'. It is now often thought of as an English specialty and, as such, is much milder. It's still delicious, though.

| | | |
|---|---|---|
| 8 cups | chicken stock | 2 L |
| 3-4 lbs | chicken, cut up | 1.5-2 kg |
| 2 | carrots, peeled and diced | 2 |
| 1 | celery stalk, chopped | 1 |
| 1 | onion, chopped | 1 |
| ¼ cup | butter | 50 mL |
| 2 tbsp | curry powder, or to taste | 25 mL |
| ¼ cup | flour | 50 mL |
| | pinch thyme | |
| 1 cup | cooked rice | 250 mL |
| 1 | tart apple, cored and chopped | 1 |
| | salt and freshly ground pepper to taste | |
| ¼ cup | table cream | 50 mL |

**Heat stock** in a large pot. Add chicken, bring slowly to a boil. Skim froth from surface with a slotted spoon and simmer about 30 minutes, until tender. Lift chicken pieces from the pot. Remove meat and set aside. Reserve stock.

**In another** large pot, sauté the carrots, celery and onion in butter. Add the curry and toss until well mixed. Stir in flour and cook briefly, stirring continuously. Don't be nervous about the way it looks; the vegetables always stick together.

**Gradually** pour in the hot stock and let simmer 30 minutes. Add the thyme, rice, apple and chicken meat. Season with salt and pepper, and cook a further 15 minutes. Swirl in the cream, heat through and serve immediately.

**Serves 6**

We find that kids prefer this soup without the curry.

# Corn Chowder

This is a hearty cold weather soup. A meal in itself. Serve with lots of hot rolls or Cornmeal Muffins (page 181).

| | | |
|---|---|---|
| 1 tbsp | butter | 15 mL |
| 3 | slices bacon, chopped | 3 |
| 1 | large onion, chopped | 1 |
| 4 | large potatoes, peeled and diced | 4 |
| 2 cups | water | 500 mL |
| 1 | bay leaf | 1 |
| 1-10 oz | can creamed corn | 1-284 mL |
| 2 cups | corn kernels (canned are just fine), drained | 500 mL |
| 1½ cups | milk | 375 mL |
| ½ cup | table cream | 125 mL |
| 1 tsp | salt | 5 mL |
| 1 tsp | chopped parsley | 5 mL |
| | croutons | |
| 4 | German-style sausages, cooked and cut in chunks (optional) | 4 |

**In a large**, heavy pot, cook bacon in butter over medium heat until softened. Add onion and cook until tender. Toss in potatoes and brown lightly.

**Pour in** the water. Add bay leaf and bring to a boil. Cover, reduce heat and simmer until tender, about 10 minutes. Gently stir in the creamed corn. Add the corn kernels, milk and cream. Heat through over medium heat. Season with salt and parsley. Garnish with croutons and fat sausage chunks.

**Serves 6**

# Cheddar Pot

This is a thick, rich, chunky, 'stick to the ribs' kind of soup. A meal on its own. Excellent after winter outings or on crisp cool autumn evenings.

| | | |
|---|---|---|
| ¼ cup | butter | 50 mL |
| 1 | small onion, chopped | 1 |
| 2 | carrots, chopped | 2 |
| 2 stalks | celery, chopped | 2 stalks |
| 3 tbsp | flour | 45 mL |
| 3 cups | chicken stock | 750 mL |
| ½ tsp | salt | 2 mL |
| 1 cup | hot milk or table cream | 250 mL |
| 2 cups | grated Cheddar cheese | 500 mL |
| | pinch cayenne, salt, white pepper to taste | |
| 1 tsp | brandy (optional) | 5 mL |

**Melt butter** in a large pan, add the chopped vegetables and cook over low heat until soft, but not brown. Blend in the flour and cook a couple of minutes. Remove from the heat and whisk in the chicken stock. Return to the heat and stir until mixture thickens, then add salt, cover and simmer about 10 minutes, until the vegetables are soft.

**Add milk**, cheese, cayenne, salt and pepper. Heat over medium heat, stirring while the cheese melts. At this point, on special occasions, add brandy.

**Serve** in warm bowls, topped with toasted croutons or crisp bacon pieces.

**Serves 4**

# Lentil Soup

A heartwarming soup quickly made from basic storecupboard items.

| | | |
|---|---|---|
| 6 cups | chicken stock | 1.5 L |
| 2 cups | red lentils | 500 mL |
| 1 | onion, roughly chopped | 1 |
| 1 | garlic clove, chopped | 1 |
| 1 tsp | curry powder | 5 mL |
| | salt and freshly ground pepper | |
| 2 tbsp | butter | 25 mL |
| | lemon slices | |
| | chopped fresh parsley | |

**Bring stock** to a boil in a large pot. Rinse lentils and add them to the pot with the onion and garlic. Simmer until lentils are tender, about 45 minutes.

**Press contents** of pot through a sieve or purée in a food mill. Return to heat. Add curry powder, season with salt and pepper to taste and simmer 5 minutes.*

**Before serving**, stir butter into hot soup. Garnish with lemon slices and chopped parsley.

**Serves 6**

In winter replace fresh vegetables with dehydrated ones; 1 tablespoon (15 mL) dehydrated onion and ¼ teaspoon (1 mL) dehydrated garlic chips.

# Feed A Crowd

**W**e can understand that people develop hearty appetites after a rigorous day of water sports or even that they might be hungry after a strenuous thirty-six holes of golf. But how can they eat so much after fishing all day, or fixing the pump or just plain loafing about? Maybe it's because food eaten in the country to the sounds of rustling leaves and calling loons just tastes so good.

Here you will find suggestions for flexible one-pot meals: the quantities may be doubled or tripled or halved, as necessary. Many of them can be completely prepared ahead of time and are useful to take along on a weekend, whether you are the host to the group or one of the guests.

Some of the dishes can be whipped up in a hurry for those times when two boatloads of smiling faces show up at the dock at dinner time; others are suitable for quieter times and special moments. They all make use of basic ingredients from the storecupboard and meats and vegetables that are readily available.

# Chicken in a Basket

A man is in general better pleased when he has a good dinner upon his table than when his wife talks Greek.
*Samuel Johnson*

An easy way to feed a crowd. Great food to take on a picnic.

| | | |
|---|---|---|
| 12 | chicken pieces, washed and well dried | 12 |
| 4 | eggs | 4 |
| 2 tbsp | table cream | 25 mL |
| 2 cups | fine breadcrumbs | 500 mL |
| 3 tbsp | grated Parmesan cheese | 45 mL |
| 1½ cups | flour | 375 mL |
| | butter | |
| | paprika | |
| | salt and freshly ground pepper | |

**Set oven** to 350°F (180°C).

**Beat eggs** well and blend with cream. Combine breadcrumbs and cheese. Dip the chicken pieces first in flour, then in the egg and cream mixture and finally coat the chicken in breadcrumbs and cheese.

**Place chicken** pieces in a large, greased baking dish or roasting pan in a single layer. Dot with butter and sprinkle generously with paprika, salt and pepper.

**Bake**, turning once, until nicely browned and crisp, about 1 hour. Eat immediately or refrigerate to eat cold.

**Serves 6**

**Sesame Chicken:** Dip chicken pieces in melted butter, then coat in a mixture of grated Parmesan cheese, breadcrumbs and sesame seeds. Place in a greased roasting pan. Dot with butter and roast in a 350°F (180°C) oven until crisp and tender, about 1 hour.

Chicken should be well cooked but still moist and juicy. When you prick the flesh the juices should run clear, with no trace of pink.

# Lemon Chicken

This dish tastes just as good made with chicken breasts that are not deboned and skinned; it's just not as refined or easy to eat. Poach an extra chicken breast in the lemony sauce to save and eat cold.

| 4 | chicken breasts | 4 |
|---|---|---|
|  | salt and freshly ground pepper |  |
| 1 | garlic clove, halved | 1 |
| ¼ cup | oil | 50 mL |
| ½ cup | lemon juice | 125 mL |
| 1 | small onion, grated | 1 |
| 1 tsp | dried thyme | 5 mL |
| ¼ cup | butter | 50 mL |

Remove skin and bone from chicken breasts. Season with salt and pepper and refrigerate until needed.

**Combine** garlic, oil, lemon juice, onion and thyme in a small bowl and leave an hour or so for flavours to blend.*

**Heat butter** in a large frying pan. Lightly brown chicken on both sides over medium-high heat. Pour lemon mixture over the chicken and cover the pan.

**Lower heat** and simmer until chicken is cooked, about 10 minutes.

**Serve** over rice or with crispy roast potatoes and a crunchy green vegetable.

**Serves 4**

# Basque Chicken

This simple recipe achieves spectacular results in a very short time. The chicken is cooked gently in tomato sauce until tender and is then topped with mozzarella cheese and olives. It looks pretty and tastes wonderful!

| | | |
|---|---|---|
| 1 tbsp | butter | 15 mL |
| 2 tbsp | olive oil | 25 mL |
| 4 | chicken pieces | 4 |
| 2 | garlic cloves, minced | 2 |
| 1 | onion, chopped | 1 |
| 1-14 oz | can tomatoes, drained | 1-398 mL |
| 1 | bay leaf | 1 |
| ½ tsp | basil | 2 mL |
| 4 | slices mozzarella cheese | 4 |
| ¼ cup | sliced green olives | 50 mL |

**Heat butter** and oil in a large heavy frying pan. Add the chicken pieces and brown on both sides over medium heat, about 10 minutes. Remove chicken and set aside.

**Toss garlic**, onion and tomatoes into the same pan. Stir about and cook until just softened. Add bay leaf and basil.

**Return chicken** to the pot. Cover and simmer until just tender, about 45 minutes.*

**Lay** the cheese slices over the chicken pieces. Sprinkle with the olives, cover and continue to simmer until cheese melts.

**Serve with** hunks of crusty bread to mop up all the juices. A good bottle of Spanish wine (Marqués de Riscal being a favourite) doesn't hurt either.

**Serves 4**

**How to peel a garlic clove:** Cut off the hard stem end. With the flat side of a knife give it a good whack (not too hard). The skin will slip off. To chop garlic: Whack the clove again to smash it. Then chop finely. To rid your hands of the smell of garlic, rub your hands with fresh lemon juice.

# Splendid Chicken Breasts

If you have time to search out special ingredients in the city, try this dish using a fine prosciutto (Italian dry cured ham) and Fontina d'Aosta, an Italian cheese with a sweet, nutty flavour. The blend of flavours will be subtle and elegant. This simpler version is also extremely good.

| | | |
|---|---|---|
| ¼ cup | butter | 50 mL |
| 6 | chicken breasts, skinned and boned | 6 |
| | salt and freshly ground pepper | |
| 6 | ham slices | 6 |
| 6 | Swiss cheese slices | 6 |
| 2 | green onions, chopped | 2 |
| ½ lb | mushrooms, sliced | 250 g |
| 2 tbsp | Madeira or sherry | 25 mL |
| ½ cup | white wine | 125 mL |

**Set oven** to 400°F (200°C).

**Heat butter** in a large frying pan. Lightly brown chicken on both sides over medium heat. Season with a pinch of salt and pepper. Cover and cook gently about 8 minutes, until chicken is tender.

**Remove** to a shallow baking dish. Cover each breast with a slice of ham and top with cheese.

**In the same** frying pan, toss onions and mushrooms and cook about 5 minutes. Spoon around chicken in baking dish.

**Add** Madeira to the pan. Stir over high heat a minute or two. Add wine and simmer the sauce a while longer. Season with salt and pepper to taste and pour around chicken.

**Ten minutes** before serving place dish in oven for flavours to blend and cheese to melt.

**Serve hot** with crispy roast potatoes and a green salad.

**Serves 6**

This chicken is also delicious when sliced and served cold.

# Beef Goulash

A friendly dish with just enough spice to make it interesting. It's versatile too; you can also use cubed veal, pork or chicken pieces.

| | | |
|---|---|---|
| 3 tbsp | oil | 45 mL |
| 1 | large onion, sliced | 1 |
| 2 tsp | paprika | 10 mL |
| | pinch cayenne | |
| 1½ lbs | lean beef, cubed | 750 g |
| 1 | garlic clove, minced | 1 |
| ½ tsp | caraway seeds, crushed (optional) | 2 mL |
| 1 tsp | salt | 5 mL |
| 2 | green peppers, seeded and sliced | 2 |
| 1 cup | canned tomatoes or 3 fresh tomatoes, chopped | 250 mL |
| 1 cup | sour cream | 250 mL |

**Heat oil** in a heavy casserole. Add onion and cook over moderate heat until soft.

**Lower heat** and sprinkle onion with paprika and cayenne. Cook briefly.

**Toss in** meat, garlic, caraway, salt, peppers and tomatoes. Cover and cook over gentle heat until meat is tender, about 1 hour. If goulash seems a little dry, add a few tablespoons water or stock.

**Stir in** sour cream and serve over egg noodles.

**Serves 4**

# Beer 'n Beef

| | | |
|---|---|---|
| 1 tbsp | cornstarch | 15 mL |
| | salt and freshly ground pepper | |

A one-pot meal. Food for Superbowls and the like.

| | | |
|---|---|---|
| 1 tsp | paprika | 5 mL |
| 1 tbsp | flour | 15 mL |
| 2 lbs | round steak or stewing beef, cubed | 1 kg |
| 1 tbsp | each oil and butter | 15 mL |
| 4 | onions, sliced | 4 |
| 1 tbsp | sugar | 15 mL |
| 1 | garlic clove, minced | 1 |
| 4 | carrots, sliced | 4 |
| 1 tsp | dried marjoram | 5 mL |
| 1-12 oz | bottle of beer | 1-341 mL |
| 1 cup | beef stock | 250 mL |
| 1 | bay leaf | 1 |
| 1 tbsp | wine vinegar | 15 mL |

**Place paprika** and flour in a plastic bag. Toss beef to coat and shake well to get rid of excess flour.

**Heat oil** and butter in a large deep pot. Brown beef well over medium-high heat. Remove and set aside.

**Add onions** and sugar to the pot. Reduce heat to medium and cook, stirring occasionally, until onions are soft.

**Toss in** garlic and carrots. Cook 5 minutes, then add the browned beef, marjoram, beer, stock and bay leaf. Bring to a boil. Lower heat and simmer, covered, until tender, about 1 hour.

**Combine vinegar** and cornstarch. Stir into pot and cook until nicely thickened. Season with salt and pepper.

**Serve with** small boiled potatoes tossed with butter and chopped parsley.

**Serves 6**

# Beef with Red Wine Sauce

A robust and tasty meal in a pot that can be made ahead. Great to take along on winter weekends.

| | | |
|---|---|---|
| 3 tbsp | flour | 45 mL |
| 1 tsp | paprika | 5 mL |
| ½ tsp | salt | 2 mL |
| 2 lbs | lean stewing beef, cut in 1" (2 cm) cubes | 1 kg |
| 2 tbsp | each oil and butter | 25 mL |
| 1 | onion, finely chopped | 1 |
| 1 | garlic clove, minced | 1 |
| 1 cup | dry red wine | 250 mL |
| 1½ cups | beef stock | 375 mL |
| 1 tbsp | red wine vinegar | 15 mL |
| ½ tsp | dried marjoram or thyme | 2 mL |
| 3 | large carrots, thinly sliced | 3 |
| ½ lb | mushrooms | 250 g |
| | freshly ground pepper | |

**Combine flour** with paprika and salt in a large bag. Toss beef pieces in mixture and shake off excess flour.

**Heat oil** and butter in a large, heavy pot. Brown the beef on all sides over medium-high heat. Remove and set aside.

**Cook onion** and garlic in the pot until tender, then stir in the browned meat. Add wine, stock, vinegar and marjoram. Bring to a boil, then lower heat, cover and simmer about 1 hour.

**Add carrots** and mushrooms and continue to simmer until meat and vegetables are tender. Season with pepper to taste.

**Serve** piping hot with simple boiled potatoes tossed in butter and fresh parsley.

**Serves 6**

# Spicy Curried Lamb

This is not for the purist who religiously bakes and blends a multitude of spices to make curry, but rather it is a quick means to a delicious end. We recommend using Madras curry powder.

| | | |
|---|---|---|
| 2 lbs | lamb or beef, cut in 1" (2.5 cm) cubes | 1 kg |
| 1 | onion, chopped | 1 |
| 1 | garlic clove, finely chopped | 1 |
| 1 tbsp | curry powder | 15 mL |
| 1 tbsp | lemon juice | 15 mL |
| 2 tbsp | oil | 25 mL |
| 2 | tomatoes, peeled, seeded and chopped (or 1-14 oz/398 mL can, drained) | 2 |
| ½ cup | water or stock | 125 mL |
| | salt and freshly ground pepper | |

**Toss meat** with the onion, garlic, curry powder and lime juice. Set aside for an hour or so.

**Strain**, reserving marinade.

**Heat oil** in a large heavy frying pan or large pot. Dry meat pieces in paper towel and brown well. Add the reserved marinade plus the other ingredients.

**Bring** just to the boil, lower heat and simmer, covered, 1½-2 hours, stirring occasionally, until sauce is rich and thick and the lamb is tender.

**Serve with** mounds of hot rice tossed with a few raisins or seasoned with a little whole cumin.

**To spice** it up, add a few hot pepper flakes or a small fresh or canned chili pepper, chopped.

### Serves 6

For a real spread, set out dishes of chutney, chopped apple, bananas, coconut, peanuts, raisins, mandarin oranges and a refreshing bowl of Sour Cream Cucumbers (see page 118) or Ginger Tomatoes (see page 115).

# Hurry Curry

For the times when all you have in the refrigerator is ground beef and you cannot face another hamburger.

| | | |
|---|---|---|
| 2 tbsp | oil | 25 mL |
| 1 | large onion, finely chopped | 1 |
| 1 | garlic clove, minced | 1 |
| 1½ lbs | ground beef | 750 g |
| 1 tbsp | curry powder | 15 mL |
| ½ tsp | turmeric | 2 mL |
| 1 | bay leaf | 1 |
| | pinch hot pepper flakes | |
| 1 tbsp | vinegar | 15 mL |
| 2 tbsp | tomato paste | 25 mL |
| | salt to taste | |
| ½ cup | water or stock | 125 mL |

**Heat oil** in a heavy frying pan and sauté onion and garlic until lightly browned. Toss in ground beef and brown.

**Now** the fun begins. Add the spices, stir 1-2 minutes, then add the remaining ingredients with enough water or stock to make the mixture moist.

**Cover pan**, lower the heat and leave to simmer 30 minutes or so.

**The same method** can be applied to cubed beef, pork, lamb or chicken pieces. Simply lengthen simmering time until the meat is tender.

**Serve with** rice (page 104) and your favourite curry condiments (page 79).

**Serves 4**

# Meatballs and Rigatoni

These meatballs will satisfy any crowd and are useful for many occasions. Make small ones to slip into a crusty roll for an Italian-style sandwich, make medium-sized ones to serve with pasta or make giant ones to serve cold sliced for a picnic.

| | | |
|---|---|---|
| 1 lb | ground meat (beef or mixture of beef, pork and veal) | 500 g |
| ½ cup | breadcrumbs | 125 mL |
| 2 | eggs, beaten | 2 |
| ¼ cup | water | 50 mL |
| 1 | small onion, minced | 1 |
| 2 tbsp | grated Parmesan cheese | 25 mL |
| 1 tbsp | finely chopped parsley | 15 mL |
| ½ tsp | salt | 2 mL |
| ¼ tsp | freshly ground pepper | 1 mL |
| 4 cups | Basic Tomato Sauce (page 82) | 1 L |
| 1 lb | rigatoni or other pasta, cooked | 500 g |

**Thoroughly combine** ground meat with breadcrumbs, eggs, water, onion, cheese, parsley, salt and pepper. Form into balls. (If you wet your hands the mixture will not stick to your fingers.)

**Heat tomato** sauce in a large, heavy pot and gently drop in the meatballs.

**Partially cover** pot and cook over low heat until meatballs are cooked through, at least 1 hour.

**Serve over** cooked pasta with a tossed green salad on the side. The meatballs are best served the next day.

**Serves 4**

**Italian-Style Sandwich:** A great lunch. Use medium crusty oval rolls, cut in half. Pile meatballs and tomato sauce on top. Top with mushrooms and hot or sweet peppers cooked in olive oil.

# Basic Tomato Sauce

This sauce has so many uses. Commit it to memory and always have the ingredients in the storecupboard.

| | | |
|---|---|---|
| 1 tbsp | oil | 15 mL |
| 1 | onion, finely chopped | 1 |
| 1 | garlic clove, minced | 1 |
| 1-28 oz | can tomatoes | 1-796 mL |
| 1-5½ oz | can tomato paste | 1-156 mL |
| ¼ tsp | dried basil | 1 mL |
| 1 | bay leaf | 1 |
| | salt and freshly ground pepper | |

**Heat oil** in a large, heavy pot. Add onion and garlic and cook over medium-high heat until softened.

**Stir in** remaining ingredients and simmer 30 minutes.

**Makes 2 cups (500 mL)**

**Spaghetti Sauce:** For a tasty spaghetti sauce, brown 1 pound (500 g) ground beef and cook up a few mushrooms and green pepper. Stir into basic tomato sauce. Stir in ½ cup (125 mL) red wine and season to taste with oregano or basil. Simmer 15 minutes.

**Chicken alla Cacciatora:** Brown chicken pieces in olive oil. Add a splash of wine and Basic Tomato Sauce. Cover pan and simmer until chicken is tender. Serve over cooked pasta with a garnish of chopped ripe olives and chopped anchovy fillets.

# Pizza

If you don't aspire to making your own pizza base (see page 183) use frozen bread dough. The frozen dough thaws slowly, over twenty-four hours, in the refrigerator or within three or four hours at room temperature.

| | pizza dough | |
|---|---|---|
| ¼ cup | Basic Tomato Sauce | 50 mL |
| | Garnishes:<br>sliced mushrooms<br>chopped green pepper<br>anchovy fillets<br>sliced olives<br>chopped bacon<br>sliced pepperoni | |
| 1½ cups | grated mozzarella cheese | 375 mL |
| 2 tbsp | grated Parmesan cheese | 25 mL |
| 1 tbsp | olive oil | 15 mL |

**Set oven** to 400°F (200°C).

**Roll** or pat pizza dough into 2 circles about 1/8" (3mm) thick and 12" (30cm) in diameter. Lay on lightly oiled pizza tins or pat into a baking tray. Pinch up edges to form a small rim.

**Brush dough** with tomato sauce and top with your choice of garnish.

**Cover with** grated cheeses and drizzle a few drops of oil over the top.

**Bake** about 20 minutes, until crust is lightly browned and cheese is melted and bubbling.

**Let pizza** rest a few minutes before slicing.

**Serves 4**

**A Picnic Pizza:** Pat pizza dough into a slightly thicker crust. Top with tomato sauce, chopped pepper, ripe olives, a scattering of grated Parmesan cheese and a few drops of olive oil. Let rest at room temperature 30 minutes or so. The dough will rise around the topping. Bake as before until crust is lightly browned and baked through.

# Tex-Mex Tacos

A fun meal for the cook and the crowd. Supply stacks of napkins: No good taco can be eaten without making a mess.

Taco shells

Tex-Mex Meat Filling

Garnishes:
shredded lettuce
chopped onion and tomato
grated Cheddar cheese
chopped hot peppers
sour cream
Guacamole (page 116)
Refried Beans (page 86)
Basic Hot Sauce

**Warm taco** shells on a baking sheet in a 350°F (180°C) oven 10 minutes.

**Prepare meat** filling and arrange a selection of garnishes and the hot sauce in separate bowls.

**Everyone** builds his own taco. First the meat filling is tucked into a taco shell and then everyone piles his favourite garnishes on top.

**Hot Tips:** Handle hot peppers with care. Remember the seeds hold most of the fire. Fingers still covered with hot pepper oil rubbed inadvertently on eyes or mouth can cause painful irritation.

The longer hot peppers sit in a sauce the more heat they release. For subtle warmth, toss hot peppers into a sauce towards the end of the cooking time.

# Tex-Mex Meat Filling

| | | |
|---|---|---|
| 2 tbsp | oil | 25 mL |
| 1 | onion, finely chopped | 1 |
| 1 | garlic clove, minced | 1 |
| 1 lb | ground beef | 500 g |
| 1 tbsp | chili powder | 15 mL |
| 1-5½ oz | can tomato paste | 1-156 mL |
| ½ cup | water | 125 mL |
| | salt and pepper | |

**In a large** heavy frying pan, sauté onion and garlic in oil until softened. Add ground beef and brown lightly. Stir in chili powder and cook briefly before adding remaining ingredients. Simmer 15 minutes.*

**Serves 4**

# Basic Hot Sauce

| | | |
|---|---|---|
| 2 cups | peeled, seeded and chopped tomatoes, or canned tomatoes, drained and chopped | 500 mL |
| 1 | medium onion, finely chopped | 1 |
| 1 | garlic clove, mashed | 1 |
| 2 tbsp | chopped green chili (or 1 tsp/5 mL hot pepper flakes) | 25 mL |
| ½ tsp | salt | 2 mL |
| | pinch ground cumin | |
| | hot pepper sauce | |

**Toss all** ingredients except the hot pepper sauce in a pot and simmer about 30 minutes. Add a few drops of hot pepper sauce if you like it fiery.* Taste first!

**Makes 1 ½ cups (375 mL)**

# Refried Beans

These are great served as a dip or as a vegetable with sour cream and guacamole. Also good with tacos or as a base for nachos.

| | | |
|---|---|---|
| 2 tbsp | oil | 25 mL |
| 1 | onion, finely chopped | 1 |
| 1 | garlic clove, minced | 1 |
| 1 | tomato, chopped | 1 |
| 1 | hot pepper, finely chopped (or ½ tsp/2 mL hot pepper flakes) | 1 |
| 1-19 oz | can kidney beans, drained | 1-540 mL |
| | salt | |

**Heat oil** in a large heavy frying pan. Add the onion and garlic and cook over medium-high heat until softened. Stir in tomato and hot pepper, and continue cooking until slightly thickened.

**Mash beans** with a potato masher. Add to the pan and cook, stirring constantly, until hot. Add salt to taste.

**Makes 1½ cups (375 mL)**

**Dried bean cookery:** Dried kidney beans when cooked from scratch have better flavour and texture than the canned variety, and are useful to keep in the storecupboard, especially in freeze-up zones. They require presoaking: Let beans stand overnight in cold water or use the quick-soak method.

**Quick-soak method:** Use 3 cups (750 mL) water for each cup (250 mL) dried beans. Bring to a full boil, boil hard 3 minutes, then remove from heat and let stand 1 hour. Return to the boil, tuck in an onion, a celery stalk or a bunch of seasoning herbs, lower heat and simmer. Cook 30 minutes if the beans are to be cooked further in a casserole, or an hour or so, until tender, if they are to be eaten as is. Season to taste before serving.

# Basic Chili

Do not be daunted by the lengthy list of ingredients. Preparation time is short; everything is tossed into the pot and left to simmer. Those with a timid palate may wish to reduce the quantity of chili powder.

| | | |
|---|---|---|
| 2 tbsp | oil | 25 mL |
| 2 | onions, chopped | 2 |
| 2 | garlic cloves, minced | 2 |
| 2 lbs | ground beef | 1 kg |
| 1 tsp | paprika | 5 mL |
| 5 tbsp | chili powder | 75 mL |
| 1 tsp | ground cumin | 5 mL |
| 1 tsp | oregano | 5 mL |
| 1 tsp | hot pepper flakes | 5 mL |
| 1-5½ oz | can tomato paste | 1-156 mL |
| 1-28 oz | can plum tomatoes | 1-796 mL |
| 1 cup | stock (or half beef stock and half beer) | 250 mL |
| 1 tsp | salt | 5 mL |
| 1-19 oz | can kidney beans | 1-540 mL |

**Heat oil** in a large, heavy pot. Add onion and garlic and cook over medium-high heat until tender.

**Add beef** and brown lightly over medium-high heat. Stir in spices and toss all together. Cook briefly.

**Add tomato** paste, tomatoes, stock and salt. Leave chili to simmer away, partially covered, about 30 minutes.

**Just before** serving, add drained kidney beans and heat through.

**Serve** in large shallow bowls with crusty bread and gobs of butter. Accompany with sour cream, corn or tortilla chips, chopped fresh tomato, green pepper and onion, and grated Cheddar cheese.

**Serves 6**

87

# Fettucine Alfredo

We often serve these creamy, cheesy noodles as a side dish with grilled loin lamb chops, fried hot peppers and a few sliced tomatoes. It also doubles as a complete meal. Just toss in a few slivers of ham and some cooked peas or broccoli.

| | | |
|---|---|---|
| ¾ lb | fettucine noodles | 325 g |
| ½ cup | butter, room temperature | 125 mL |
| 1 cup | table cream | 250 mL |
| 1 cup | grated Parmesan cheese | 250 mL |
| | freshly ground pepper | |
| 1 tbsp | finely chopped parsley | 15 mL |

**Cook fettucine** and drain. Return to pot and set over low heat. Add ¼ of the butter and a little of the cream. Stir well. Add a few tablespoons of cheese.

**Continue** to stir in remaining butter, cream and cheese. The sauce will be thick, creamy and oh so rich! Absolutely superb.

**Sprinkle** with pepper and parsley when serving.

**Serves 4**

For 2, halve the recipe.

**To chop parsley:** Place parsley sprigs in the bottom of a cup. Cut with scissors until finely chopped.

# Spaghetti Carbonara

We like to serve Spaghetti Carbonara with grilled steaks or lamb chops, instead of potatoes. A large romaine salad with a vinaigrette dressing makes this a perfect meal.

| 8 | bacon or prosciutto slices, chopped | 8 |
|---|---|---|
| 3 tbsp | olive oil | 45 mL |
| ¾ lb | spaghetti | 325 g |
| 4 | eggs, beaten | 4 |
| ½ cup | grated Parmesan cheese | 125 mL |
| | freshly ground pepper | |
| | finely chopped parsley | |

**Fry bacon** or prosciutto in oil until soft. Set aside. Cook the spaghetti. Drain and place in a large pot over low heat.

**Add** the bacon fat, beaten eggs and grated Parmesan cheese. Mix quickly and well.

**Stir in** bacon, pepper and parsley. Toss well. Serve immediately.

**Serves 4**

If you are lucky enough to have some prosciutto on hand, it adds an authentic flavour.

**Pasta Tips:** Everyone always cooks too much pasta, or too little. Make a circle with your thumb and forefinger roughly the size of a quarter. A bunch of spaghetti to fill the circle will make 1 serving (2-3 ounces/ 50-75 g).
To avoid last-minute panic, cook pasta until just tender. Add 2-3 cups (500-750 mL) cold water. This halts the cooking without cooling the pasta and gives you some breathing time to get yourself organized.

# Linguine with Clam Sauce

A great dish from the storecupboard.

| | | |
|---|---|---|
| 2-5 oz | cans baby clams | 2-142 g |
| 1 | garlic clove, minced | 1 |
| 1 | onion, finely chopped | 1 |
| 2 tbsp | butter | 25 mL |
| ½ cup | white wine | 125 mL |
| 1 tbsp | parsley, chopped | 15 mL |
| | salt and freshly ground pepper | |
| ¾ cup | whipping cream | 175 mL |
| 1 tbsp | flour | 15 mL |
| ¾ lb | linguine, cooked (or spaghetti) | 325 g |

**Drain clams**, reserving liquid.

**Sauté garlic** and onion in butter, in a large, heavy frying pan, until tender. Toss in clams and cook 2 minutes. Add clam juice, wine, parsley and seasonings. Cover and simmer 10 minutes.

**Gently stir** in ½ cup (125 mL) cream and bring to a boil. Blend the remaining cream with the flour and stir the mixture into the sauce. Cook, stirring, over medium heat until sauce thickens and adjust seasoning.*

**Combine creamy**, hot, clam sauce with hot cooked linguine in a large, warm bowl and serve promptly with baskets of fresh crusty bread for mopping up your plates.

**Add chunks** of other cooked shellfish to the sauce if you are lucky enough to have some around.

**Serves 4**

**Linguine with Red Clam Sauce:** Follow the recipe for white clam sauce, but add 1 pound (500 g) peeled, seeded and chopped tomatoes (or a 14-oz/398 mL can, drained) when frying the onion and garlic, and leave out the cream and flour. Add ½ teaspoon (2 mL) sugar and ½ teaspoon (2 mL) dried basil to the seasonings.

# Pasta Primavera

This Italian classic has many variations. It involves some basic preparation (chopping of vegetables) and some last-minute cooking. However, everything is dumped into one pot and tossed about for a few minutes to heat. That's it!

| | | |
|---|---|---|
| 1 tbsp | each oil and butter | 15 mL |
| 1 | onion, chopped | 1 |
| 1 | garlic clove, minced | 1 |
| 4 cups | assorted vegetables: asparagus is superb, broccoli, a few carrots, cauliflower, zucchini, mushrooms, trimmed and chopped in equal-sized pieces | 1 L |
| ½ cup | chicken stock | 125 mL |
| ½ cup | whipping cream | 125 mL |
| ¾ lb | fettucine noodles, cooked and drained | 325 g |
| 1 cup | grated Parmesan cheese | 250 mL |

**Use** a giant pan with a good sturdy bottom (a wok works perfectly). Heat the oil and butter. Toss in the onion and garlic and cook over medium-high heat until softened.

**Add** the remaining vegetables. Toss about until just hot. Add the stock and cream. Cover and bring to a boil. Simmer 2-3 minutes. The veggies should still have a nice crunch.

**Finally**, stir in the pasta and cheese. Serve at once.

**A leafy** green salad or a few sliced tomatoes drizzled with oil, lemon juice and oregano makes a good side dish.

**Serves 6**

# The Great Noodle Stack-Up

Otherwise known as lasagne. Noodles layered with almost anything make a great feed-a-crowd dish. Here's a tried and true version to start with, but try some of the other varieties. You'll soon be inventing your own.

| | | |
|---|---|---|
| 1 recipe | Spaghetti Sauce with or without wine (page 82) | 1 recipe |
| 9 | lasagne noodles, cooked | 9 |
| 12 oz | mozzarella cheese, thinly sliced | 375 g |
| 2 cups | cottage cheese | 500 mL |
| ½ cup | grated Parmesan cheese | 125 mL |

**Set oven** to 350°F (180°C).

**Lightly grease** a 9" x 13" (3 L) baking dish. Spoon a little of the spaghetti sauce on the bottom. Cover with a layer of lasagne. Pile on ⅓ of the sauce and a layer of mozzarella. (The secret to slicing mozzarella cheese is to use a cheese slicer.) Top with ⅓ of the cottage cheese and sprinkle with Parmesan cheese. Repeat two more times.

**Cover with** foil and bake 30 minutes. Uncover and let cook some more, until crunchy all over.

**Serves 8**

**Fabulous Fillings:** In addition to spaghetti sauce, use meatballs (page 81). Use ricotta cheese instead of cottage cheese for a lighter texture. Or, combine 2 cups (500 mL) cottage cheese or ricotta with 2 eggs. Beat well. Mix in 1 cup (250 mL) cooked, drained and chopped spinach. Season with a good pinch of basil. Layer with tomato sauce, mozzarella and Parmesan. Or, layer with tomato sauce, mozzarella, Parmesan and the Ratatouille (page 102) or Kitchen Sink Vegetables (page 98).

**No-stick Noodles:** Rinse lasagne noodles and keep in warm water with 1 tablespoon (15 mL) oil. This prevents them from sticking together.

# Savoury Meat Pie

Bake the filling between layers of pastry to make a savoury pie to take along on a picnic. Or to eat at home, cover with a lid of packaged puff pastry or make a topping of biscuit mix.

| | | |
|---|---|---|
| 1 lb | lean pork, minced | 500 g |
| ½ lb | veal, minced | 250 g |
| 1 | onion, chopped | 1 |
| 1 | potato, peeled and grated | 1 |
| 1 | garlic clove, mashed | 1 |
| 1 tsp | salt | 5 mL |
| | freshly ground pepper | |
| ¼ tsp | each dried thyme and ground allspice | 1 mL |
| ½ cup | water | 125 mL |
| | pastry for a double crust pie (page 182) | |
| | cream or beaten egg | |

**Set oven** to 450°F (230°C).

**Combine** all ingredients except pie crust in a large pot. Simmer, uncovered, about 45 minutes, stirring occasionally.

**Set aside** to cool. Skim off excess fat or stir to distribute fat evenly.

**Line** a pie plate with pastry, fill with meat mixture and cover with another pastry layer. Seal and pinch edges, brush top with a little cream or beaten egg and cut vents in pastry lid to allow steam to escape.

**Bake** 10 minutes at 450°F (230°C), then lower heat to 350°F (180°C) and continue baking until pastry is golden, about 35 minutes.

**Serves 6**

# Sweet and Sour Spareribs

| | | |
|---|---|---|
| 2 lbs | spareribs | 1 kg |
| ¼ cup | soy sauce | 50 mL |
| 1 tbsp | honey | 15 mL |
| 1 | garlic clove, minced | 1 |
| ½ tsp | ground ginger | 2 mL |
| 1 | recipe Sweet 'n Sour Sauce | 1 |

**Set oven** to 325°F (160°C).

**Ask** the butcher to cut the spareribs into thirds lengthwise. Cut into bite-sized pieces. Mix together the soy sauce, honey, garlic and ginger. Toss in the ribs and marinate 1 hour.

**Drain** ribs. Place in a baking dish. Cover and bake about 45 minutes.

**Serve** with Sweet 'n Sour Sauce.

**Serves 4**

# Sweet 'n Sour Sauce

| | | |
|---|---|---|
| 1-10 oz | can mandarin oranges or canned pineapple | 1-284 mL |
| 1 cup | vinegar | 250 mL |
| 1 cup | sugar | 250 mL |
| 2 tbsp | soy sauce | 25 mL |
| ½ tsp | ground ginger | 2 mL |
| 2 tbsp | cornstarch mixed with 2 tbsp (25 mL) water | 25 mL |
| 2 | green onions, finely chopped | 2 |
| 1 | green pepper, cut in thin strips | 1 |
| 2 tbsp | sweet relish (optional) | 25 mL |

**Drain** the fruit and reserve juice. Mix together the fruit juice, vinegar, sugar, soy sauce and ginger. Bring to a boil and simmer 5 minutes. Add the cornstarch mixture and cook until nicely thickened. Stir in the green onion, green pepper, fruit, and relish, if you like. Heat through.

**Makes 2 cups (500 mL)**

# Crab Supper Pie

Equally fine for brunch or lunch.

| | | |
|---|---|---|
| 1-9" | unbaked pastry shell (page 182) | 1-23 cm |
| 1-6 oz | can crabmeat | 1-170 g |
| 1 cup | grated Swiss cheese (about 4 ounces/125 g) | 250 mL |
| 2 | chopped green onions | 2 |
| 3 | eggs | 3 |
| 1 cup | table cream | 250 mL |
| ½ tsp | grated lemon rind | 2 mL |
| ½ tsp | salt | 2 mL |
| | freshly ground pepper | |
| | pinch each dry mustard and grated nutmeg | |
| ¼ cup | sliced almonds | 50 mL |

**Set oven** to 350°F (180°C).

**Drain crabmeat** and separate into chunks.

**Sprinkle cheese** evenly over bottom of pastry shell. Top with crabmeat and green onions.

**Combine eggs**, cream, lemon rind and seasonings and pour over crabmeat. Top with sliced almonds.

**Bake** about 45 minutes or until pastry is golden and filling is set. As with all quiches, allow pie to rest a few minutes before serving.

**Crisp greens** and a tomato salad complete the meal.

**Serves 4**

**Seafood Bake:** A can of lobster (well drained) can be substituted for the crab. Flash-frozen shrimps are good too. Toss them into lightly salted boiling water. As soon as the water returns to the boil test to see whether they are ready. Drain immediately and rinse under cold-water tap.

95

# Ways With Vegetables

**W**henever we sit down to a plate piled high with tender asparagus bathed in lemony egg dressing, we wonder why we bother with meat at all. Most of our ways with vegetables will, in fact, make a light meal with the addition of some fresh crusty bread to mop up the good juices.

Our choice of fruit and vegetables to take along on a trip is largely determined by how well they stand up under the stress and strain of long hours wedged in a car trunk, standing about on a dock in the noonday sun and being tossed about in an open boat (even people sometimes find these experiences trying!). Usually refrigerated space is very limited at a country place; we, therefore, suggest how to prepare vegetables in marinades that retain their flavour and crunch for hours without refrigeration, and ways to prepare interesting dishes from a lifeless carrot or other vegetables that have seen better days.

If there is a sunny spot close by, plant a clump or two of parsley, mint and chives; with luck they will come up year after year, and you will have their fresh flavour at hand whenever you need it.

# Kitchen Sink Vegetables

A cucumber should be well sliced, and dressed with pepper and vinegar, and then thrown out as good for nothing.
*Samuel Johnson*

A useful dish when all you have is an assortment of tired, old vegetables and a boatload of unexpected guests shows up at suppertime. To a base of olive oil, onion, garlic and ripe tomatoes, add whatever vegetables you have; just don't overcook them.

| | | |
|---|---|---|
| 3 tbsp | olive oil | 45 mL |
| 1 | large onion, sliced | 1 |
| 2 | garlic cloves, mashed | 2 |
| 2 | green peppers, seeded and sliced | 2 |
| 2 | zucchini, scrubbed and sliced | 2 |
| ½ lb | green beans, trimmed and cut in half | 250 g |
| | cauliflower or broccoli flowerets (optional) | |
| 1 | hot pepper, seeded and sliced | 1 |
| 3 | large ripe tomatoes, quartered | 3 |
| | salt and freshly ground pepper | |
| | fresh or dried basil | |
| | chopped fresh parsley | |
| | grated Parmesan cheese (optional) | |

**Heat oil** in a large, heavy frying pan. Add onion and cook over medium-high heat until soft. Add garlic, peppers, zucchini, beans and cauliflower and toss in oil 5 minutes or so.

**Gently stir** in remaining ingredients except Parmesan and cook mixture, covered, about 15 minutes.

**Remove lid** and continue simmering until excess juices have cooked away.

**Serve hot** and sprinkle with grated Parmesan cheese if you like.

**Serves 4 to 6**

# Lemon Potatoes

Potatoes roasted until golden and crisp with a variety of flavourings are simple to make for two or twelve. Excellent to serve with just about any meat. Quantities are for each serving.

| | | |
|---|---|---|
| 1 | potato | 1 |
| 1 tbsp | butter | 15 mL |
| | grated lemon rind | |
| 1 tsp | lemon juice | 5 mL |
| 1 tbsp | grated Parmesan cheese | 15 mL |
| | pinch paprika | |

**Set oven** to 350°F (180°C).

**Peel potatoes** and cut into smallish chunks.

**Melt butter** in a roasting pan. (Choose a pan in which the potatoes can cook in a single layer.) Add potatoes and toss in melted butter with the other ingredients.

**Roast** about 45 minutes, until potatoes are crisp and golden on the outside and tender within. Turn them over once or twice during cooking so they brown on all sides.

**Sprinkle** with salt and serve at once.

**Rosemary Potatoes:** Instead of using butter, toss potatoes in olive oil and flavour with garlic and a liberal pinch of dried rosemary. Roast potatoes at 400°F (200°C) instead of 350°F (180°C).

**Potato in Foil:** Cut one piece of foil for each potato and butter or oil lightly on the shiny side. Place a potato (peeled or unpeeled) on each piece. Rub with butter, sprinkle with parsley, paprika, salt and pepper. Wrap well and bake in a 400°F (200°C) oven until tender, about 45 minutes.

# Potato Baskets

Make these ahead and just reheat in a medium oven when ready to eat.

| 4 | large baking potatoes | 4 |
|---|---|---|
| 2 tbsp | butter | 25 mL |
| 2 tbsp | table cream or milk | 25 mL |
| ½ cup | grated Cheddar cheese | 125 mL |
| 1 tsp | chopped parsley | 5 mL |
| | salt and freshly ground pepper to taste | |
| | paprika | |

**Set oven** to 400°F (200°C).

**Wash potatoes** and prick the skins with a fork. Bake until tender, about 45 minutes.

**Cut potatoes** in half lengthwise when cool enough to handle. Scoop out the insides, leaving the shells intact. Mash the potato with the butter, cream, cheese, parsley, salt and pepper, and spoon mixture back into skins. Sprinkle with paprika.*

**Reheat** in 400°F (200°C) oven when ready to serve, about 20 minutes.

**Serves 4 to 8**

**A Memorable Moment:** A friend of ours said that one of her fondest memories was biting into a stuffed Potato Basket. The taste was euphoric, which was understandable considering the build-up—she had just driven 400 miles in long weekend traffic with nothing to eat since lunch; had traversed a road that stunt drivers would have problems tackling; had then been piled into a rather small wooden boat with a chug-a-lug motor and tossed about in a rough sea. Naturally she was famished.

# Scalloped Tomatoes

A tasty side dish to any meat.

| | | |
|---|---|---|
| 1 | medium onion, finely chopped | 1 |
| ¼ cup | butter | 50 mL |
| 1 cup | breadcrumbs | 250 mL |
| | salt and freshly ground pepper to taste | |
| ½ tsp | oregano | 2 mL |
| 8 | tomatoes, peeled and sliced | 8 |
| 1 cup | grated Cheddar cheese | 250 mL |

**Set oven** to 350°F (180°C).

**In a frying pan,** cook the onion in butter over medium heat until softened. Remove and set aside. Add breadcrumbs to the pan and brown lightly; you may need a little more butter. Season with salt, pepper and oregano.

**Layer tomatoes,** onion, cheese and breadcrumbs in a greased baking dish. (Make 2 or more layers, if you have to.)* Bake 40 minutes, until top is golden and tomatoes are tender.

**Serves 6**

**How to chop an onion:** Peel the onion and cut it in half lengthwise. Place flat side down on chopping board. Make 3 or 4 horizontal cuts in the onion, leaving the stem end intact. Make similar cuts towards the stem end, parallel to the table. Now cut at right angles, vertically, and onion will be chopped in small squares.

# Ratatouille Niçoise

We include this classic medley of Mediterranean vegetables, even though it is a bit fussy to prepare, because we love it and no summer would be complete without it.

| | | |
|---|---|---|
| 1 | medium-sized eggplant | 1 |
| 4 | zucchini | 4 |
| 6 | ripe tomatoes | 6 |
| 2 | onions | 2 |
| 2 | green peppers | 2 |
| | olive oil | |
| | salt and freshly ground pepper | |
| | pinch fresh or dried thyme | |
| 2 | garlic cloves, mashed | 2 |

| | | |
|---|---|---|
| 1 tsp | dried basil | 5 mL |
| 1 tbsp | chopped fresh parsley | 15 mL |

**Prepare** the vegetables. This is the tiresome part so enlist some helpers. Peel the eggplant and cut into sections approximately the size of your thumb. Scrub zucchini and cut likewise. Peel, seed and chop tomatoes. Peel and slice onions and seed and slice peppers.

**Use 2** large heavy frying pans at once to shorten preparation time.

**Heat** 3 tablespoons (45 mL) olive oil in one frying pan. Cook onions and peppers over medium heat about 10 minutes, then add tomatoes, a little salt, pepper and a pinch of thyme. Raise heat, cook 2-3 minutes more and set aside.

**Meanwhile** in the other frying pan, heat 6 tablespoons (100 mL) olive oil over high heat. Lightly brown the eggplant pieces, lifting them out with a slotted spoon as they are ready. Brown the zucchini in the same way.

**In a heavy** pot combine the tomato mixture and the browned vegetables and add garlic, basil and parsley.

**Cook** over medium heat until hot, stirring gently. Lower heat and simmer 20 minutes. Best prepared ahead to allow time for flavours to mingle.

**Serve hot** or at room temperature with roasted or grilled meats. Excellent also tucked into an omelette or as a base for baked eggs.

**Serves 4 to 6**

**Vegetables for disorganized cooks:** If the vegetables are almost cooked and the rest of the meal isn't ready, don't worry. Remove from heat and drain. When ready to serve, toss in a little butter over medium heat until warmed through. Stir in a little sour cream and sprinkle with toasted walnuts or almonds. Flavour with a good squeeze of lemon and finely chopped herbs.

> **Tip:** Slice or chop eggplant and zucchini an hour or so before cooking. Sprinkle with salt and set in a sieve so that some of the bitter juices drain away. If tomatoes have tough skins drop them into boiling water for the count of 10, then plunge them into cold water. Scoop out core and cut a cross at other end. The skin then slips off easily. To remove seeds and excess water from tomatoes, cut in half crosswise and squeeze gently.

# Versatile Rice Pilaf

A pilaf is one of the best 'put your feet up' dishes. Initially a few flavourings are tossed in butter with the rice. Liquid is added and then the pot is left to cook away quietly.

| 2 tbsp | minced onion | 25 mL |
| 1 | garlic clove, minced | 1 |
| 2 tbsp | butter | 25 mL |
| 1 cup | long grain converted white rice | 250 mL |
| 2 tsp | ground turmeric | 10 mL |
| 2 cups | chicken stock | 500 mL |
| 1 | bay leaf | 1 |
| ½ tsp | salt | 2 mL |

**In a saucepan** over medium heat, sauté onion and garlic in 1 tablespoon (15 mL) of butter until softened. Stir in rice and turmeric and toss and cook for a few minutes.

**Add stock**, bay leaf and salt and bring to a boil. Cover the pot, lower heat and simmer steadily until liquid is absorbed and rice is tender, 25 minutes.

**Before serving**, toss lightly with remaining butter.

**Serves 4**

**Orange Pilaf:** Proceed as above but omit garlic and turmeric. Sauté 1 chopped green pepper with the onion. Flavour with grated orange rind and for the liquid use 1 cup (250 mL) each orange juice and water. Sprinkle with slivered almonds before serving. Serve with grilled lamb chops, chicken or fish.

**Spanish Pilaf:** Proceed as above but sauté 1 chopped tomato and 1 chopped green pepper with the onion. Use 1 cup (250 mL) stock and 1 cup (250 mL) tomato juice as the cooking liquid. Serve with grilled pork or chicken.

**Brown Rice Pilaf:** Proceed as above but increase the liquid ½ cup/125 mL (i.e. 2½ cups/625 mL chicken stock) and lengthen the cooking time to about 45 minutes. Wonderful with lamb, especially if you toss in a few lightly sautéed sliced mushrooms.

**Never-fail Rice:** The following method always works. Use long grain converted rice. Fill a large pot with water (4 to 6 cups/1-1.5 L). Bring to a rolling boil. Toss in 1 cup (250 mL) rice and a pinch of salt. Don't cover. Place over medium heat. Set timer to 14 minutes and disappear. When the bell rings, return and drain. The rice will be perfect. Prepare any old time. When you want to reheat rice, place it in a colander over a pan of hot water. Place a makeshift lid on top! It doesn't have to fit exactly. Leave to steam over low heat. In 10-15 minutes, the rice will be hot and fluffy but still firm.

# Sweet Carrot Bites

Plain old carrots made remarkable.

| | | |
|---|---|---|
| 8 | medium carrots, peeled | 8 |
| 2 | bacon slices, chopped | 2 |
| 2 tbsp | maple syrup | 25 mL |
| | salt and freshly ground pepper | |

**Slice carrots** in rounds. Steam if possible or boil until tender but still crunchy. Drain well.

**While carrots** are cooking, sauté bacon in a small frying pan. Remove and set aside. Drain off all but 1 tablespoon (15 mL) of bacon fat.

**Toss carrots** in bacon fat with bacon bits and maple syrup. Season with salt and pepper. Delicious!

**Serves 4**

# Brandied Carrots

Often the simplest is the best.

| | | |
|---|---|---|
| 8 | medium carrots, peeled | 8 |
| 1 tbsp | butter | 15 mL |
| 1 tbsp | sugar | 15 mL |
| 1 tsp | finely chopped parsley | 5 mL |
| | squeeze lemon juice | |
| 1 tsp | brandy | 5 mL |

**Cook carrots** until tender but still crunchy. Drain.

**Return to pot** and toss with remaining ingredients.

**Serves 4**

# Curried Vegetable Pot

A tasty satisfying vegetable dish that can be prepared from the storecupboard at any time of the year. Delicious with curries and roast or grilled lamb.

| | | |
|---|---|---|
| 1 cup | yellow or green dried split peas | 250 mL |
| 2 cups | water | 500 mL |
| 1 tsp | salt | 5 mL |
| 1 tbsp | oil | 15 mL |
| ½ | medium onion, chopped | ½ |
| 1 | garlic clove, minced | 1 |
| ½ tsp | ground turmeric | 2 mL |
| ½ tsp | curry powder | 2 mL |
| | juice of ½ lemon | |

**Rinse split peas** and combine with water and salt in a saucepan. Bring to a boil and cook, covered, over medium heat until soft, about 30 minutes. Leave as is, or mash.

**Cook onion** and garlic in hot oil in a frying pan over medium-high heat until soft and lightly browned. Stir in turmeric and curry powder and cook 1 minute more. Add spicy mixture to the cooked split peas and squeeze lemon juice over top.

**Serves 6**

In wintertime, the fresh vegetables may be replaced with dehydrated ones. Add 1 tablespoon (15 mL) dehydrated onion and ¼ teaspoon (1 mL) dehydrated garlic chips to the split peas while they are cooking. In the last few minutes stir in turmeric, curry powder and 1 tablespoon (15 mL) butter.

# Mayonnaise

It works like a charm if all the ingredients are at room temperature.

| | | |
|---|---|---|
| 2 | egg yolks | 2 |
| 1 tbsp | lemon juice or wine vinegar | 15 mL |
| ½ tsp | Dijon-style or dry mustard | 2 mL |
| ½ tsp | salt | 2 mL |
| ¼ tsp | freshly ground pepper | 1 mL |
| ¾ cup | olive or salad oil | 175 mL |

**Place egg yolks**, half the lemon juice, the mustard, salt and pepper in a bowl. Whisk the mixture vigorously until lemon-yellow and lightly thickened.

**Start to blend** in the oil very slowly, with nerves of steel, drop by drop, until the mixture emulsifies and thickens. Add remaining lemon juice and season to taste.

**Makes 1 cup (250 mL)**

One tablespoon (15 mL) boiling water whisked into the completed mayonnaise will keep the mixture stable and prevent it from separating.

---

**Tip:** If mayonnaise begins to fall apart, don't panic. Take a clean bowl and another egg yolk and gradually add the separated mayonnaise, beating constantly. It's as simple as that!

# Broccoli Bonanza

A salad made with pasta can easily serve as a meal. This is quite substantial as is, but you could easily add sliced cooked chicken breasts, slices of ham, salami or cooked shrimp.

| | | |
|---|---|---|
| 1 | bunch broccoli | 1 |
| 1½ cups | pasta (shells or macaroni) | 375 mL |
| 1 | large (or 2 medium) red onions, thinly sliced | 1 |
| ½ tsp | hot pepper flakes | 2 mL |
| 1 | garlic clove, minced | 1 |
| ¾ cup | mayonnaise | 175 mL |
| | salt and freshly ground pepper to taste | |
| 1 tbsp | lemon juice | 15 mL |

**Cut and break broccoli** into flowerets (not too small). Cook until tender and drain.

**Boil pasta** until tender and run under cold water. Drain well.

**Toss** broccoli, pasta and remaining ingredients together in a large bowl. Note that garlic has a stronger taste when raw; add with caution. Refrigerate overnight.

**Just before** serving, adjust seasoning and add another squeeze of lemon juice if necessary.

**Serves 4**

Raw vegetable salads often call for mild and sweet Spanish onions or flavourful, red-skinned onions. If you do not have them on hand, substitute a few fresh green onions, trimmed, sliced length-wise and finely chopped.

# Artichoke Heart Salad

In downtown Toronto there is an old-fashioned Italian grocery store called Pasquale's, which is justly famous for its artichoke heart salad. This is a facsimile.

| 2-14 oz | cans artichoke hearts | 2-398 g |
|---|---|---|
| 1 | red-skinned onion, finely sliced | 1 |
| 1 | celery stalk, finely chopped | 1 |
| | a few black olives | |
| 1 recipe | Savoury Italian Dressing | 1 recipe |
| 1 tsp | paprika | 5 mL |
| | chopped fresh parsley | |

**Rinse and drain** artichoke hearts and combine with onion, celery and olives.

**Pour** Savoury Italian Dressing over vegetables. Sprinkle generously with paprika and parsley. Chill until serving.

**Serves 6**

## Savoury Italian Dressing

| ½ tsp | salt | 2 mL |
|---|---|---|
| 1 | garlic clove, mashed | 1 |
| 1 tbsp | wine vinegar | 15 mL |
| 3 tbsp | olive oil | 50 mL |
| ¼ tsp | hot pepper flakes | 1 mL |

**Combine salt** and garlic with vinegar. Whisk in olive oil and pepper flakes.

**Makes ¼ cup (50 mL)**

**Storing olives and canned chilies:** Drain off preserving liquid. Place in glass jars and add oil to cover. Store in covered jars in refrigerator.

# Copper Coins

Pickle taste and texture without the preserving kettle.

| | | |
|---|---|---|
| 1 lb | carrots, peeled and cut in rounds | 500 g |
| 1-7½ oz | can tomato sauce | 1-213 mL |
| ¼ cup | oil | 50 mL |
| ½ cup | sugar | 125 mL |
| 1/3 cup | vinegar | 75 mL |
| ½ tsp | dry mustard | 2 mL |
| ½ tsp | Worcestershire sauce | 2 mL |
| | salt and freshly ground pepper to taste | |
| 1 | small green pepper, chopped | 1 |
| 1 | onion, chopped | 1 |

**Cook carrots** until tender but still crunchy.

**In a small** saucepan, combine tomato sauce, oil, sugar, vinegar, mustard, Worcestershire sauce, salt and pepper. Bring just to a boil and simmer until sugar is dissolved.

**Mix sauce** with the cooked carrots, green pepper and onion. Cover and marinate in the refrigerator 2-3 days. Keeps well 1-2 weeks.

**Serve** as a side dish with grilled meats or as part of an antipasto.

**Serves 4 to 6**

# Summertime Salad

In a large bowl, combine torn romaine lettuce, washed and dried well; a thinly sliced Spanish or red onion; a can (10-oz/284 ml) of mandarin oranges, drained, or slices of peeled oranges; and toasted almonds. Toss with Vinaigrette. (page 114).

# Chickpea Salad

A quickie. Drain 1 can (19 oz/540 mL) chickpeas. Rinse under cold water and drain again. Toss with Vinaigrette (page 114), some finely chopped onion, green and/or red pepper and a little celery, if available.

# Marinated Cauliflower

This serves well as either a summer vegetable or a refreshing crunchy salad.

| | | |
|---|---|---|
| 1 head | cauliflower | 1 head |
| ¼ cup | white wine vinegar | 50 mL |
| ½ tsp | salt | 2 mL |
| ¼ cup | olive oil | 50 mL |
| 2 | garlic cloves, mashed | 2 |
| 1 tsp | dried oregano | 5 mL |

**Cut and break** the cauliflower into flowerets. Marinate it in vinegar and salt overnight.

**Drain** well. Toss with oil, garlic and oregano. Let stand one hour or more.

**Serves 4**

# Asparagus with Tangy Egg Dressing

This is a superb salad. The asparagus is firm and crunchy and the dressing sharp and creamy.

|  | juice of 2 lemons |  |
|---|---|---|
| 1 lb | asparagus, cleaned and ends removed | 500 g |
| 1 recipe | Tangy Egg Dressing | 1 recipe |

**Fill** a large pot with water. Add lemon juice. Bring to a full boil.

**Toss in** asparagus. Return to boil. Let asparagus boil 5 seconds. Drain and chill.

**To serve**, arrange on a platter and spoon the dressing on top.

**Serves 2**

## Tangy Egg Dressing

| 3 tbsp | olive oil | 45 mL |
|---|---|---|
| 1 tsp | salt | 5 mL |
| ½ tsp | freshly ground pepper | 2 mL |
| 1 tsp | Dijon-style mustard | 5 mL |
| 1 tbsp | red wine vinegar | 15 mL |
| 1 tsp | lemon juice | 5 mL |
|  | yolks of 2 hard-boiled eggs, sieved |  |

**Blend** all ingredients well and pour over vegetables.

**Makes ½ cup (125 mL)**

**Tip:** The best way to eat asparagus is with your fingers. Just grab the stalk and eat tip first. (Envision yourself being fed grapes in ancient Rome.)

# Marinated Tomatoes

Possibly our favourite salad when local tomatoes are sweet and ripe. A delicious side dish for simple grilled or barbecued meats, and a fine lunch with the quick addition of chunks of Greek feta or Swiss cheese and a handful of olives. Serve with garlic bread to mop up the tangy juices.

| | | |
|---|---|---|
| 1 | Spanish or red-skinned onion | 1 |
| 6 | large ripe tomatoes | 6 |
| | pinch each sugar, salt and freshly ground pepper | |
| 1 tsp | celery seed | 5 mL |
| ½ cup | Vinaigrette | 125 mL |
| | fresh chopped herbs (basil or dill, chives and parsley) | |

**Peel and slice** onion and separate into rings. Slice tomatoes. Arrange on a large platter.

**Sprinkle with** sugar, salt, pepper and celery seed. Pour the vinaigrette over vegetables.

**Scatter herbs** on top. Cover platter with plastic wrap and refrigerate 1-2 hours.

**Serves 6**

## Vinaigrette

| | | |
|---|---|---|
| ½ tsp | salt | 2 mL |
| 2 tbsp | wine vinegar | 25 mL |
| ¼ tsp | freshly ground pepper | 1 mL |
| ½ tsp | Dijon-style mustard | 2 mL |
| 6 tbsp | olive oil | 75 mL |

**In a small** bowl, whisk the salt into the vinegar; stir in pepper and mustard. Add the oil slowly, beating until thick and creamy.

**Makes ½ cup (125 mL)**

# Ginger Tomatoes

The advantage to this salad is that it still tastes good with bland winter tomatoes. Use fresh ginger if possible.

| | | |
|---|---|---|
| 4 | tomatoes, quartered | 4 |
| 2 | medium onions, cut in strips | 2 |
| 1-inch | piece fresh ginger root, peeled and minced (or ½ tsp/ 2 mL ground ginger) | 2.5 cm |
| 1 tsp | whole cumin seed | 5 mL |
| | lemon juice to taste | |
| | salt and freshly ground pepper to taste | |

**Toss** all ingredients together and let sit for a while so all the flavours are drawn out.

**Serves 4**

Excellent with spicy dishes.

**To store fresh ginger root indefinitely:** Scrape skin off the root, wash and pat dry. Place in a jar and cover with dry sherry. Cover with a tight-fitting lid and store in the refrigerator. The ginger-laced liquor also makes a wonderful flavouring ingredient.

## Last-Minute Chutney

To make a quick chutney: Cook up an onion and green pepper in oil. Add a tablespoon (15 mL) each curry powder and brown sugar, a 14-oz/398 mL can peaches, drained and chopped and 2 tomatoes, chopped. Cook, stirring often, 10 minutes. Chill or, if in a panic, stick in the freezer to cool quickly.

**Makes 1½ cups (375 mL)**

# Guacamole

Serve with tortilla or corn chips as a dip, or with Tex-Mex Tacos (page 84) as a salad.

| | | |
|---|---|---|
| 2 | large avocados, peeled and chopped | 2 |
| 2 | medium tomatoes, finely chopped | 2 |
| 1 | small onion, finely chopped | 1 |
| 2 | canned green chilies or Tabasco to taste | 2 |
| 1 tbsp | lemon or lime juice | 15 mL |
| | salt and freshly ground pepper to taste | |

**In a small** bowl, mash together 2 tablespoons (25 mL) each of the avocados, tomato and onion with the chilies. (Use a blender if you wish.) Stir in the remaining avocado, tomato and onion. Add lemon juice and seasonings.

**Serves 4**

**To keep guacamole green:** Spread a thin layer of sour cream on top and refrigerate. Mix just before serving. Or, mash avocado with ½ cup (125 mL) canned lima beans.

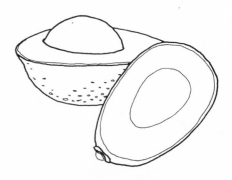

# Sweet Cucumbers

For a more exotic version, add a teaspoon (5 mL) of grated fresh ginger to the dressing.

| 2 | cucumbers | 2 |
|---|---|---|
| 1 tsp | salt | 5 mL |
| ¼ cup | vinegar | 50 mL |
| 3 tbsp | sugar | 45 mL |

**Cut cucumbers** in half and dig out the seeds. Slice thinly. Sprinkle with ½ teaspoon (2 mL) salt. Let stand 15 minutes. Squeeze cucumbers gently to get rid of excess water.

**Combine** remaining salt, vinegar and sugar and mix until sugar is dissolved. Toss gently with cucumber. Chill until ready to serve.

**Serves 4**

**Tip:** With skinny mild English cucumbers, there is no need to peel or seed. The squat, fat cucumbers are best if both skin and seeds are removed. Slice cucumber in half lengthways and scoop away seeds with a spoon. Then slice and use in salads, soups, dips or even as a vegetable.

# Sour Cream Cucumbers

This dish tastes better if made a day ahead to allow flavours to mingle.

| | | |
|---|---|---|
| 2 | cucumbers | 2 |
| ½ tsp | salt | 2 mL |
| 2 tsp | sugar | 2 mL |
| 2 tbsp | vinegar | 25 mL |
| 1 cup | sour cream | 250 mL |
| 1 tsp | celery seed | 5 mL |
| 2 tbsp | chopped fresh dill | 25 mL |
| 1 tbsp | chopped chives or green onion | 15 mL |

**Slice cucumbers** wafer thin.

**Combine** salt and sugar with vinegar. Stir into sour cream and add celery seed, dill and chives.

**Drain** cucumbers of excess liquid and gently stir into sour cream mixture.

**Refrigerate** at least a couple of hours.

**Serves 4**

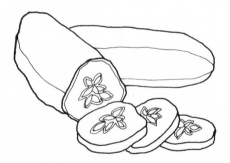

# Vegetables that Crunch

A colourful vegetable salad that will keep two or three days in the refrigerator. Makes a great lunch or snack anytime.

| | | |
|---|---|---|
| 1 cup | olive oil | 250 mL |
| 1½ cups | red wine vinegar | 375 mL |
| ¼ cup | sugar | 50 mL |
| ½ tsp | freshly ground pepper | 2 mL |
| 1 tsp | salt | 5 mL |
| 1 | garlic clove, mashed | 1 |
| 2 | green peppers, seeded and chopped into chunks | 2 |
| 1 | cauliflower, broken into flowerets | 1 |
| 2 | red-skinned (or regular) onions, thinly sliced | 2 |
| 1 lb | mushrooms, quartered | 500 g |
| ½ lb | black or green olives | 250 g |
| 1 pint | cherry tomatoes, halved | 500 mL |

**Combine** oil, vinegar, sugar, pepper, salt and garlic in a small pot and bring mixture to a boil.

**Pour dressing** over prepared vegetables.

**Toss** together and refrigerate several hours.

**Serves 4**

**Peppers with Pizzazz:** The contrasting colour of red and green peppers makes a spectacular presentation. Cut the tops and skin from green and red peppers. Halve, remove seeds and trim away ribs. Cut in very thin strips. In a glass bowl, toss together with vinaigrette and a little chopped fresh or dried basil.

# Greek Salad

An all-time summer favourite when the tomatoes are rich and sweet. Food for company. Just serve with a plate of thinly sliced ham and salami, a chilled white wine and some good bread.

| | | |
|---|---|---|
| 1 | large onion, thinly sliced | 1 |
| 2 | tomatoes, sliced | 2 |
| 1 | cucumber, thinly sliced | 1 |
| 1 | leaf lettuce | 1 |
| ¼ lb | feta cheese | 125 g |
| ¼ lb | Greek olives | 125 g |
| 3 tbsp | olive oil | 45 mL |
| | juice of ½ lemon | |
| | salt and freshly ground pepper | |
| | oregano | |

**Separate** onion slices into rings. Arrange attractively with tomatoes and cucumber on a bed of lettuce.

**Sprinkle with** the feta cheese, olives, oil, lemon juice, salt, pepper and oregano. Chill 30 minutes.

**Serves 4**

# Spinach Salad

Spinach holds up particularly well under the strain of cottage traveling.

| | | |
|---|---|---|
| 4 | bunches, fresh spinach (or 1-10 oz/284 g bag) | 4 |
| 4 | bacon slices | 4 |
| 1 | hard-boiled egg, sliced | 1 |
| 2 tbsp | grated Parmesan cheese | 25 mL |
| 1 recipe | Vinaigrette (page 114) | 1 recipe |

**Wash spinach** and dry well. Remove stems and tear into large pieces.

**Cook bacon** until crisp. Drain and crumble.

**Toss** all the ingredients together in a large bowl.

**Serve with** grilled steaks or lamb chops or just on its own with lots of Italian Cheese Bread (page 53).

**Serves 4**

Toasted slivered almonds, cashews and sliced raw mushrooms make nice additions.

# Caesar Salad

Caesar never made it like this! The dressing is made ahead and then tossed with the lettuce before serving.

| | | |
|---|---|---|
| 1 | romaine lettuce | 1 |
| 3 | anchovy fillets, finely chopped | 3 |
| ½ tsp | Dijon-style mustard (or ¼ tsp/1 mL dry mustard) | 2 mL |
| 1 | garlic clove, mashed | 1 |
| 4-5 shakes | Worcestershire sauce | 4-5 shakes |
| 2 | egg yolks | 2 |
| | juice of ½ lemon | |
| ¾ cup | olive oil | 175 mL |
| | croutons | |
| | grated Parmesan cheese | |

**Wash lettuce** and dry well. Tear into large pieces. Chill well.

**Mix anchovies**, mustard, garlic and Worcestershire sauce in the bottom of a large bowl. Grind with the back of a spoon until a paste is formed. Use a couple of croutons to help work into a paste.

**Add egg** yolks. Mix well. Then the lemon juice. Beat in the oil a little at a time. Believe it or not you've just made mayonnaise!

**Just before** serving, toss with the lettuce, croutons and Parmesan cheese.

**Serve with** a thick juicy steak and a full red wine.

**Serves 4**

Garlic overdose? Chew parsley, nature's freshener.

**Croutons:** Cut bread into cubes. Melt 1-2 tablespoons (15-25 mL) butter in a heavy frying pan. Add 2-3 garlic cloves, peeled and cut in half. Toss in the bread cubes and stir until well coated. Place on a cookie sheet and bake in a 300°F (150°C) oven until crisp, about 10 minutes. Remember to toss out the garlic cloves before adding the croutons to the salad.

# Sweet Vinegar Coleslaw

Crisp and refreshing. A salad that stands up under stress.

| | | |
|---|---|---|
| 1 cup | sugar | 250 mL |
| 1 cup | cider vinegar | 250 mL |
| ⅔ cup | oil | 150 mL |
| 1 tsp | Dijon-style mustard | 5 mL |
| ½ tsp | celery salt | 2 mL |
| ¼ tsp | salt | 1 mL |
| ¼ tsp | freshly ground pepper | 1 mL |
| 1 | large cabbage, shredded | 1 |
| 2 | large carrots, grated | 2 |
| 1 | medium pepper, grated or finely chopped | 1 |
| 1 | medium onion, grated or finely chopped | 1 |

**Combine** the sugar, vinegar, oil, mustard, celery salt, salt and pepper. Blend.

**Toss together** with the remaining ingredients and refrigerate overnight. Keeps fresh in refrigerator for a week.

**Serves 6**

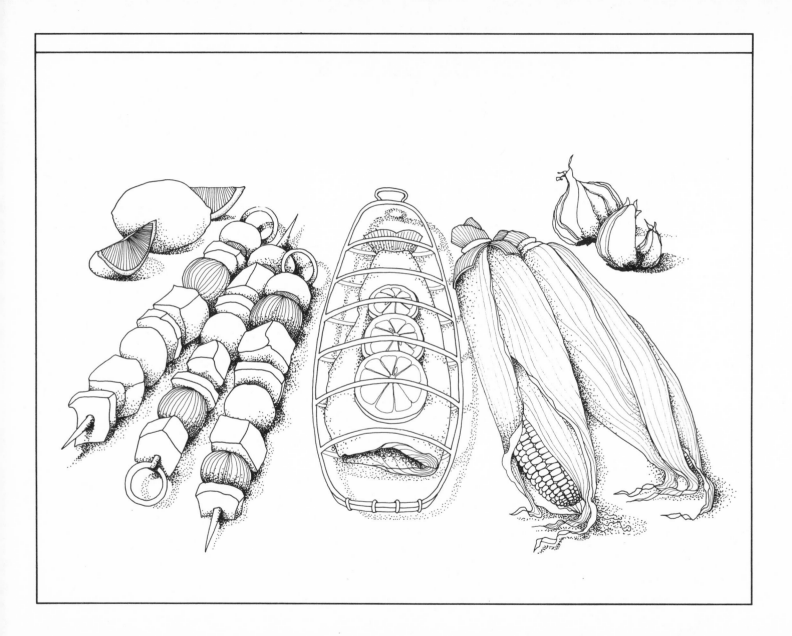

# Fresh Air Cooking

It's eight o'clock in the evening and *someone* was supposed to have started the fire ages ago. *Someone* forgot. Everyone is starving, the food is waiting and the coals are only lukewarm. By nine o'clock the mosquitoes are out in full force and the fire is perfect. It's dark out and no one can find the flashlight; the meat ends up raw or charred and the salad, prepared hours ago, is now a disaster. But by candlelight, far from the madding crowd, it all tastes wonderful—and that's what barbecuing is all about anyway.

Cooking out of doors is an essential part of summer; it's easy, it's fun and the food always tastes so good. We prefer to bring out the natural flavours of grilled meat and fish by subtle means, so we usually avoid overpowering sauces and seasonings. We leave meats to sit for a while in aromatic marinades or we use a herb-flavoured basting sauce during cooking. And then, of course, we feast on all the mouthwatering accompaniments; crisp pickles, crunchy garlic bread and hot buttered corn on the cob.

We also include here our method for roasting a pig over the coals; it's a feast that makes for a real party.

# Barbecue Basics

...let us also not forget that it is always dangerous to quarrel with your cook... if the cook is useless there is no point in keeping her; but if she is, on the whole, satisfactory, why change?

*X. Marcel Boulestin*
*(1931)*

We include a few suggestions based on our experience of many cookouts—a primer, rather than a thesis, on barbecuing.

**If you are about to cook** on a fancy jet-propelled, propane-powered barbecue unit we urge you to study the operating manual that came with it before you begin: a simple step but an essential one if you want to make use of all the built-in features and get good cooking results.

**For the simple barbecue**, charcoal briquets seem to be the most convenient fuel. Keep them dry and make sure you have enough. Twenty to twenty-five briquets should generate sufficient heat to grill fast-cooking meats (lamb chops, hamburgers, etc.) for six people. To maintain heat over a long cooking period, when cooking a roast of meat on a spit, for example, have on hand forty briquets or more. Add new coals around the fire and push them to the centre as the others die away.

**Start the fire** with a pile of dry twigs or pine needles, a bullrush dipped in coal oil, a couple of small cubes of solid fuel barbecue starter or, if you have an accessible electrical outlet, an electric fire starter. Mound the coals in a pyramid shape at first. When they are glowing and showing grey ash around the edges spread them in an even layer, set grill in place and, when the grill is hot, begin cooking. This procedure always takes longer than you think, at least thirty minutes.

**A makeshift chimney** set on top of the coals creates a draft, which speeds up the fire at the start. A large juice or coffee can, both ends removed, with holes punched around the bottom, serves the purpose. Be sure to remove the hot can with tongs or a pair of pliers and set it down in a safe place to cool.

# Barbecue Tips

**Lightly oil** grill to prevent meat from sticking.

**Dry meat** with paper towels in order for it to brown well. Trim away excess fat to reduce smoking and flare-up.

**One test of the heat** of the fire recommended by the fearless is to hold your hand about 4 inches from the coals. A count of 5 before you are forced to withdraw is a rough indication of perfect grilling heat, about 350°F (180°C).

**First sear meat** close to the coals on both sides then raise grill to about 7 inches (18cm) from fire and continue the cooking, turning meat from time to time to brown and cook it evenly.

**Baste** with sauces or marinades only during the last minutes of cooking or the meat will char on the outside before it is cooked through.

**Splash** a little water on the coals should flare-up occur.

**Sprinkle meat** with salt at the end of cooking so that the juices are not drawn out and lost. For the same reason use tongs, not a fork, to turn meat.

**Heavy-duty foil** is very useful when barbecuing. Use dull side out to wrap vegetables or fish.

**Hickory or maple chips** tossed on the coals add a real woodsy flavour.

**Fast-cooking**, popular items for the barbecue include beef steaks, lamb chops, beef or lamb patties or shish kabobs, sausages, fish and shellfish. Unless you have a fairly sophisticated barbecue unit on which you can control the heat we suggest you partially cook chicken or pork in the oven and finish the cooking with a brief period over the coals. These meats require thorough cooking and frequently turn out dry and lifeless after a lengthy period over hot coals.

**To cook large roasts** or whole birds over coals use a rotisserie, spit or a covered barbecue. The only sure way to know whether these cuts are sufficiently cooked is to use a meat thermometer. The tiny thermometer with a narrow stem that registers internal meat temperature instantly is ideal. Most people cannot resist poking around with the barbecue so our advice to the everyday cook is to hand over the tongs and disappear to take a swim or a snooze.

# Honey Garlic Chicken Wings

| | | |
|---|---|---|
| 2 lbs | chicken wings | 1 kg |
| 1 recipe | Honey Marinade | 1 recipe |

**Wipe chicken** wings with paper towels. Chop off wing tips; they usually burn before the rest of the wing is cooked. Cut wings into two pieces at the joint.

**Toss with** honey marinade. Leave several hours.*

**To cook**, remove wings from marinade and grill over coals. Turn frequently until the wings are evenly browned and cooked through. Brush with marinade mixture after 30 minutes or so.

**Wings** may also be cooked in a 350°F (180°C) oven approximately 45 minutes.

**Serve with** rice and a crisp salad.

**Serves 4**

## Honey Marinade

Try this sweet-spicy marinade with spareribs or cubes of pork as well.

| | | |
|---|---|---|
| 2 tbsp | oil | 25 mL |
| 2 tbsp | liquid honey | 25 mL |
| 1 tbsp | red wine vinegar or lemon juice | 15 mL |
| 1/3 cup | soy sauce | 50 mL |
| 1 tsp | fresh ginger root, minced (or 1/2 tsp/ 2 mL ground ginger) | 5 mL |
| 1 | garlic clove, minced | 1 |
| 1 tbsp | green onion, chopped | 15 mL |

**Combine** ingredients and mix well.

**Makes ¾ cup (175 mL)**

**Barbecue Tip:** Keep a bowl of water on hand when barbecuing in order to douse the flames that occasionally erupt from the fat on meat dripping onto the coals. Simply sprinkle water on the coals with fingertips until flames subside. Do not pour water on the meat.

# Barbecued Chicken Tandoori Style

During the summer months, barbecued food never seems mundane, but it's fun to try slightly different methods.

| 8 | chicken pieces | 8 |
| 1 recipe | Tandoori Marinade | 1 recipe |

**Spoon marinade** over chicken pieces and refrigerate until ready to use, preferably overnight.*

**Remove chicken** from marinade and barbecue about 7 inches (18 cm) from heat, basting with the sauce.

**Serve with** bowls of rice and chutney.

**Serves 4**

Chicken may also be baked in a 350° F (180° C) oven 45 minutes or cooked for 30 minutes and finished on the barbecue.

## Tandoori Marinade

| 1 | onion | 1 |
| 1 | garlic clove | 1 |
| 2 tbsp | lemon juice | 25 mL |
| 1 tbsp | curry powder | 15 mL |
| ½ tsp | ground cinnamon | 2 mL |
| 1 tsp | salt | 5 mL |
| 1 tsp | paprika | 5 mL |
| 1 cup | Balkan-style plain yogurt | 250 mL |

**Chop onion** and garlic very finely and whisk together with remaining marinade ingredients.

**Makes 1¼ cups (300 mL)**

# Barbecued Spareribs

The secret to succulent barbecued ribs is to braise them gently on top of the stove before putting them on the grill.

| | | |
|---|---|---|
| 4 lbs | lean spareribs | 2 kg |
| 2 tbsp | oil | 25 mL |
| 1 | onion, sliced | 1 |
| 1 | lemon, sliced | 1 |
| ½ cup | water, stock or red wine | 125 mL |
| 1 | bay leaf | 1 |
| 1 recipe | Tangy Barbecue Sauce | 1 recipe |

**Cut spareribs** into serving pieces and trim away excess fat. Heat oil in a large skillet and lightly brown the ribs.

**Add remaining** ingredients, cover and cook over low heat approximately 45 minutes, until ribs are tender. Remove and set aside. This preparation may be completed ahead of time and the ribs set, covered, in the refrigerator until ready to barbecue.*

**When ready** to serve, brush the surface of prepared ribs with Tangy Barbecue Sauce and set them on a rack over moderate coals. Cook 10 minutes. Turn, baste well with sauce and continue to cook on the other side.

**Serves 4**

**Tip:** Have beekeeper's hat on hand for cooking outdoors. It's indispensable when the mosquito bombardment begins. Since the hat includes a net over your face, the most important consideration is that you can still drink beer through it. We have tested this diligently over the summer and our findings are affirmative.

# Tangy Barbecue Sauce

Use this sauce for ribs, steaks, lamb chops or chicken.

| | | |
|---|---|---|
| 2 tbsp | butter | 25 mL |
| 1 | onion, finely chopped | 1 |
| 1 | garlic clove, minced | 1 |
| 1 tsp | curry powder | 5 mL |
| 1-14 oz | can tomato sauce | 1-398 mL |
| ¼ cup | ketchup | 50 mL |
| | dash Tabasco | |
| 1 tsp | Worcestershire sauce | 5 mL |
| 2 tbsp | brown sugar | 25 mL |
| 2 tbsp | vinegar | 25 mL |
| ½ tsp | dried basil or oregano | 2 mL |
| | salt and freshly ground pepper to taste | |

**Melt butter** in a heavy pot. Add the onion and garlic and cook over medium heat until soft. Stir in curry powder. Toss in the remaining ingredients, mix well and simmer 15 minutes.

### Makes 2 cups (500 mL)

Use any extra sauce for dipping. Stir in some chopped fresh pineapple (or canned, in a pinch) for a wonderful flavour.

## Last-Minute Barbecue Sauce

In a small pan heat together 1 cup (250 mL) commercial barbecue sauce and ¼ cup (50 mL) honey. Baste meat with sauce while grilling and serve extra sauce on the side for dipping.

**Barbecued Sausages:** Italian sweet or hot sausages are particularly good on the barbecue. Prick the sausage skins several times, set in a pot and cover with cold water. Bring to a boil. Lower heat and simmer 10 minutes. Drain. Make 3 slits on the side of each sausage. Brown over the coals, basting with Tangy Barbecue Sauce until the skin is crispy.

# The Utah Burger

In Park City, Utah you can ski halfway down the hill and stop at an open-air grill for a freshly charcoal-broiled hamburger. There are huge pots of melted cheese to ladle over the whole thing. This makes an interesting and messy change from the regular cheeseburger.

| | | |
|---|---|---|
| 4 | hamburger patties, grilled | 4 |
| 4 | kaiser rolls, toasted and buttered | 4 |
| 3 cups | grated Cheddar cheese | 750 mL |
| ½ cup | flour | 125 mL |
| 1 cup | milk | 250 mL |
| 1 tsp | butter | 5 mL |
| 1 tsp | dry mustard | 5 mL |
| | Tabasco and Worcestershire sauce to taste | |

**While** the hamburgers are on the grill, toss cheese with flour in a bowl.

**Heat milk** and butter in a large saucepan. Gradually stir in the cheese.

**Cook and stir** until nicely thickened. Stir in the dry mustard. Season to taste with Tabasco and Worcestershire sauce.

**Place grilled** burgers on rolls, smother with cheese sauce and add your favourite toppings. A knife and fork may be in order!

**Serves 4**

The cheese sauce makes a great spread for crackers. Simply refrigerate to cool.

> **Tip:** How can you tell whether your hamburger or steak is ready? Serve one to the person who ordered the rarest and take a look.

# Candlelight Burger

The name says it all.

| 2 lbs | lean ground beef | 1 kg |
|---|---|---|
| 2 tbsp | dry white vermouth | 25 mL |
| | butter | |
| | salt and freshly ground pepper | |
| 4 | warmed crusty rolls | 4 |
| | Herb-Garlic Butter | |
| 4 | Swiss cheese slices | 4 |
| 4 | smoked ham slices | 4 |

**Combine** the meat, vermouth and seasonings and form into 4 patties.*

**Brush** with butter and broil medium-rare.

**Split rolls** and spread both halves with Herb-Garlic Butter. Place a cheese slice on the bottom half, cover with the broiled burger, the smoked ham and the top of the bun.

**Serves 4**

## Herb-Garlic Butter

Use on broiled steaks or lamb chops, or use to make garlic bread. Great as a stuffing for mushrooms.

| ½ cup | softened butter | 125 mL |
|---|---|---|
| 1 | garlic clove, minced | 1 |
| 1 tsp | finely chopped parsley | 5 mL |
| | salt to taste | |

**Combine** the above ingredients. Roll in foil and refrigerate or freeze until needed. Use other herbs for flavour, such as basil, oregano or chives.

**Poor Man's Chicken Kiev:** When you make hamburgers, take a spoonful of hard Herb-Garlic Butter or creamed blue cheese and tuck it inside.

# Pearl Geneen's Crunchy Cucumber Pickles

Pearl Geneen owns a marvellous cookware store in downtown Toronto. Her quick, crispy pickles are wonderful with steaks and burgers.

| | | |
|---|---|---|
| 1 cup | vinegar | 250 mL |
| 3 tbsp | sugar | 45 mL |
| 2 tsp | mustard seed | 10 mL |
| 1 tsp | peppercorns | 5 mL |
| 4 | garlic cloves | 4 |
| 4 | bay leaves | 4 |
| 2 tsp | prepared mustard | 10 mL |
| 2 | lemon slices | 2 |
| ½ tsp | salt | 2 mL |
| 2 | cucumbers | 2 |

**In a small** pan, bring all ingredients, except cucumbers, to a boil. Cook 5 minutes.

**Slice cucumbers** in eighth lengthwise. Cut slices in two, place in a shallow dish and cover with the marinade.

**Cover** and refrigerate 24 hours. These keep well for a week.

**Makes 2 cups (500 mL)**

# Lamb Chops on the Grill

Thick juicy charcoal-broiled lamb chops are perhaps our very favourite barbecued food. They are almost as good when cooked under the broiler.

| | | |
|---|---|---|
| 8 | loin lamb chops (1-1½"/2-3 cm thick) | 8 |
| 1 recipe | Lemon Marinade | 1 recipe |

**Coat lamb chops** in marinade and let stand covered 2 hours or overnight.*

**Remove chops** from marinade and cook over medium coals, about 6 minutes a side, until nicely browned on the outside but still pink and juicy on the inside.

**Serve with** fresh tomato slices, a crisp green salad and lots of Herb-Garlic Bread (page 53).

**Serves 4**

## Lemon Marinade

| | | |
|---|---|---|
| ¼ cup | oil | 50 mL |
| 2 tbsp | lemon juice | 25 mL |
| 1 | onion, chopped | 1 |
| 1 | garlic clove, chopped | 1 |
| | dash Tabasco | |
| | dash Worcestershire sauce | |
| ¼ tsp | dry mustard | 1 mL |
| | freshly ground pepper | |
| 1 | bay leaf | 1 |

**Combine** the ingredients in a small bowl and mix well.

**Makes ½ cup (125 mL)**

# Shish Kabobs

How can anything this simple seem so special? Shish kabobs are occasion food. They are fun to put together, lovely to look at and delicious to eat. We like to use two or three different marinades, but any one will do the trick.

| | | |
|---|---|---|
| 1½ lbs | lamb, pork, or beef, cut in 1½"/4 cm cubes | 750 g |
| | Soy, Lemon and/or Spicy Chili Marinade | |
| | enough vegetables for 8 skewers: quartered onions, chunks of green or red pepper, whole mushrooms, cherry tomatoes or tomato quarters | |
| | bacon slices (optional) | |

**Toss meat** in the marinades. (If using three kinds of meat, be sure to keep the pork separate as it takes slightly longer to cook.) Cover and refrigerate at least 2 to 3 hours.

**Place bowls** of meat, vegetables and skewers on the table. Get the company to help put them together or do them yourself ahead of time.

**Alternate** pieces of meat with vegetables. The tomatoes should go at the ends of the skewers since they cook the fastest. Place 4 or 5 pieces of meat on each skewer. A small slice of bacon between each piece of meat adds a tasty flavour.* Cover with plastic wrap until ready to use.

**Cook** shish kabobs on a hot barbecue about 4" (10 cm) from the heat. Turn and baste frequently.

**Serve with** a large Spinach Salad (page 121) and Crisp Garlic Bread (page 53).

**Serves 4**

# Soy Marinade

| | | |
|---|---|---|
| ½ cup | soy sauce | 125 mL |
| 1 | garlic clove, mashed | 1 |
| ¼ cup | granulated sugar | 50 mL |
| | juice of 1 lemon | |
| 2 tbsp | oil | 25 mL |

**Combine** the ingredients in a small bowl and mix well.

**Makes 1 cup (250 mL)**

**Traveling Shish Kabobs:** Cut meat and toss in marinade. Place in well-sealed containers. That way the mess is done at home. All you need to do is skewer the meat with vegetables when you're ready to eat.

# Spicy Chili Marinade

| | | |
|---|---|---|
| 2 tbsp | oil | 25 mL |
| 2 tbsp | lemon juice | 25 mL |
| ½ cup | canned tomato sauce | 125 mL |
| 1 tbsp | brown sugar | 15 mL |
| 2 tbsp | chili powder | 25 mL |
| | freshly ground pepper | |

**Combine** all the ingredients in a small bowl and mix well.

**Makes 1 cup (250 mL)**

# Barbecued Pork on a Stick

This is a simplified version of Indonesian saté; tasty morsels of meat cooked over charcoal on wooden skewers. It works equally well with pieces of chicken or beef. If possible use a Japanese soy sauce (Kikkoman) or an Indonesian (Conimex). When using the regular stuff, add an extra tablespoon of sugar to the marinade.

| | | |
|---|---|---|
| 2 lbs | pork, cubed (¾" / 2 cm pieces) | 1 kg |
| 1 recipe | Indonesian-Style Marinade | 1 recipe |
| 1 recipe | Peanut Sauce | 1 recipe |
| | bacon slices (optional) | |

**Toss pork** cubes in a large bowl with marinade. Let stand covered overnight.

**Drain and slide** meat onto wooden skewers (4 pieces to a stick). If you wish you can slip a piece of bacon between each slice.*

**Barbecue** about 4" (10 cm) from coals or broiler.

**Serve with** Peanut Sauce, extra soy sauce, Ginger Tomatoes (page 115) and steamed rice.

**Serves 4**

## Indonesian-Style Marinade

| | | |
|---|---|---|
| ¼ cup | soy sauce | 50 mL |
| 1 tbsp | brown sugar | 15 mL |
| 2 tbsp | lemon juice | 25 mL |
| 2 tbsp | oil | 25 mL |
| 1 tsp | curry powder | 5 mL |
| 1 tsp | ground ginger | 5 mL |

**Combine** the ingredients in a small bowl and mix well.

**Makes ½ cup (125 mL)**

## Peanut Sauce

| 1 cup | roasted peanuts | 250 mL |
|---|---|---|
| 1 | onion, minced | 1 |
| 1 | garlic clove, minced | 1 |
| 1 tsp | paprika | 5 mL |
| ½ cup | water | 125 mL |
| 2 tbsp | lemon juice | 25 mL |
| 2 tbsp | soy sauce | 25 mL |

**Combine** all the ingredients in a blender jar and whirl until creamy. Pour into a saucepan and cook until thickened, 5 minutes. Spoon a bit of sauce over the barbecued pork.

**Makes 1 cup (250 mL)**

## Barbecued Corn

**Strip husks** down to the stem of corn, but do not remove. Pull off the silk. Brush kernels with soft butter and sprinkle with salt and freshly ground pepper. Replace husks around corn, wrap in a double thickness of heavy-duty foil and twist ends. Barbecue over hot coals about 25 minutes, turning frequently.

## Barbecued Potatoes

**Scrub skins** of medium-sized white potatoes and rub with soft butter. Wrap in a double thickness of heavy-duty foil. Barbecue over hot coals, about 45 minutes, turning now and again.

# Heavenly Barbecued Trout (or other small fish)

| 4 | trout | 4 |
|---|---|---|
| 2 tbsp | flour | 25 mL |
| | salt and freshly ground pepper to taste | |
| ½ cup | butter, melted | 125 mL |
| | lemon or lime wedges (optional) | |

**Clean trout** and wipe with a damp cloth. Toss fish into a plastic bag containing flour seasoned with salt and pepper; dip the floured trout in melted butter.

**Set fish** in a hinged grill basket (or a well-greased grill with a small grid) and cook over the coals about 4-5 minutes on each side, basting with melted butter, until the skin is crisp and lightly browned and the flesh flakes.

**Serve** immediately with more butter, lemon or lime wedges and freshly ground pepper.

**Serves 4**

Small boiled new potatoes and a fresh green vegetable complete the dish but we sometimes like to feast on sweet, freshly caught fish all by themselves.

**Tip:** A hinged grill basket is a handy wire contraption that resembles an old-fashioned popcorn maker or a campfire toaster. Small fish and delicate fish fillets can be easily turned over the coals when secured between the grills.

# How to Roast a Pig

First find your pig. This is usually the most difficult task. Try your local farmer's market, pork producers' association or ask a good butcher. A weight of between 20 and 40 pounds (10 and 20 kg) is a good size for a small spit. Make sure the pig is well cleaned. If you purchase the pig a few days beforehand, store it in a cool place, loosely wrapped.

**Organize the pit** and spit the day before cooking and have contingency plans for rain. A piece of metal sheeting can serve as a rain splash if necessary.

**The day of the roast**, start the coals 1-1½ hours before you're ready to cook. If you don't have a barbecue pit, dig a shallow pit in the ground and surround it with rocks or bricks. You may line it with several thicknesses of foil or bricks if there are lots of tree roots in the area. Use 20-30 pounds (10-15 kg) of charcoal to begin with. Light the charcoal, using small twigs and branches or charcoal starter. Wrap thin plywood boards in heavy-duty foil and place around the pit to act as wind protectors and heat reflectors.

**When you've started the coals**, prepare the pig. This may mean a quick dip in the lake or a good washing with clean towels. Pat the pig well dry, using paper towels. Place the pig on a spit and secure it well. Our spit consists of a stainless steel pipe. The supports have joints to lower and raise it, depending on what we're cooking. We have drilled holes in the pipe at 6" (15 cm) intervals. We slide a shish kabob skewer through the holes in the pipe and then into the pig's hocks. Another skewer is placed through the shoulder at the hips and the back hocks. The front and back hocks are wired in a circular fashion, using medium-gauge wire. Wire is looped in a figure 8 around the middle skewers. Now lay the pig on its side and stuff the cavity around the spit. Use a basic turkey dressing tossed with a little chopped apple and bacon, and sea-

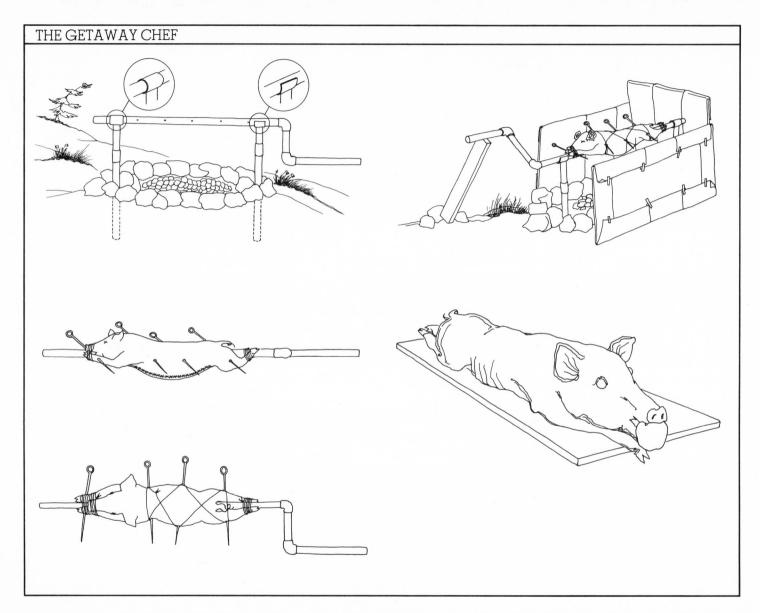

soned with thyme. Sew up the cavity using a large needle and string or secure it with large turkey skewers.

**Cook, basting with oil**, about 1½-2′ (45-60 cm) from coals, rotating every 4-5 minutes. Have a crowd of people gathered round for all this manual labour. Prop the ends of the spit with a block of wood to support it as you turn the pig. After about 2-3 hours, the skin will start to bubble and crackle. Wrap several pieces of foil around the centre of the pig, shiny side out since you want the heat deflected. Continue cooking until done. To test when done, insert a meat thermometer in the thickest part of the leg. It should register 170° (80°C). This will usually take 4-6 hours, depending on the size of the pig. It's best to have guests close at hand in case the roast pig is ready early.

**Remove from spit**. The skin is the best part so make sure everyone gets a piece. Eating the pig Tom Jones fashion is rather fun. If you wish to carve it, the best thing to use is common sense. The shoulder and haunch may be carved like a roast. The centre ribs may be cut between the bones.

**Serve with** corn on the cob, juicy thick tomato slices, bread and Sweet Vinegar Coleslaw (page 123).

20 lb (10 kg) pig serves approximately 10 and takes about 4 hours to cook
30 lb (15 kg) pig serves approximately 20 and takes about 5 hours to cook
40 lb (20 kg) pig serves approximately 30 and takes about 6 hours to cook

# Catch or Cache

**F**ather had just finished cleaning the day's catch; eighteen beautiful fillets of smallmouth bass were lined up neatly on the fish table. A minute later they had disappeared. A seagull was perched on a rock nearby looking very pleased with himself. We had a can of beans that night.

Many vacation places are close to water and like it or not we all have to face cooking the catch at one time or another. We have all had to stretch two or three perch to feed a crowd and cook the big one when it didn't get away.

We have cooked fish in almost every way possible: sautéed gently in butter for breakfast or made into fish burgers for lunch. At dinnertime we often light into a pile of fish and chips or dine on poisson au beurre blanc.

Unless a particular fish is specified, all recipes may be made with fish from the sea or freshwater fish. Most are good with seafood, too!

Also, for those who may be faced with the bag of an amateur hunter, we suggest a few simple ways for preparing game.

# A City Person's Guide to Cleaning Fish

The only difficult part of cleaning a fish is reading the instructions. Whew!

**Getting off the hook:** For small fish, up to 4 lbs/2 kg, grab the fish firmly behind the head. If you are timid about the whole business carry an oven mitt with you. With fingers or a small pair of pliers hold the tip of the hook and bend it away from the barbed end. Don't be afraid to use force.

**Filleting:** The first rule is to use a razor-sharp flexible knife. You cannot clean fish with a dull knife. Place the fish on a wooden board, belly side down. Hold firmly with left hand.

Cut through to the backbone just behind the head. Now cut through the flesh behind the two sides and lower fins to sever the head. Cut through the backbone. Pull the head from the body. The insides will come away, too. With the sharp edge of the knife facing up, run the tip under the skin along one

side of the back fin, three-quarters the length of the fish, and then slant the knife down and along the backbone to release the tail. Beer break! Swat the fly! Proceed.

Working along the backbone, sharp side of the knife down, carefully cut the flesh away from the bone. There is a rounded cage at the front that is a little awkward to get around. Repeat on other side and pull or cut away the backbone. You will now have two fillets, with the skin on, looking a little like a butterfly. Cut in half.

With skin side down, hold the tip of the tail. Run the knife, angled down and forward, between the flesh and the skin. The fillet will come away smoothly and easily. Wash well. And there you have it; two beautiful fillets.

In truth, the first time you'll probably have two hacked up pieces of flesh not really resembling anything. Don't worry, it will come.

**To prepare fish for baking:** Scale and gut the fish. Using a serrated knife brush at right angles firmly against the scales. They will come away easily. Remember all fish do not have scales (e.g. trout, salmon). To gut a fish you may proceed in the same manner as in cleaning fish, removing the head. If you wish to leave the head on simply run the tip of your knife along the belly from the anus to just under the front fins. Remove the innards and wash well.

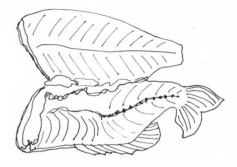

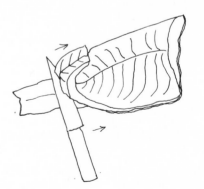

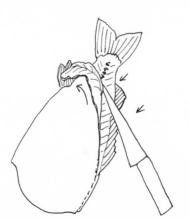

# English Style Fish and Chips

Tom and Huck fried the fish with bacon and were astonished, for no fish had ever seemed so delicious before. They did not know that the quicker a fresh water fish is on the fire after it is caught, the better it is, and they reflected little upon what a sauce open-air sleeping, open-air exercise, bathing and a large ingredient of hunger make, too.

*By the Campfire,*
*Mark Twain*

Keep your old newspapers and serve everyone their fish and chips wrapped in newsprint with the salt shaker and malt vinegar bottle close at hand. Old and young (not to mention the dish-washers) get a kick out of it.

## The Fish:

| | | |
|---|---|---|
| 1 cup | prepackaged pancake mix | 250 mL |
| ¾ cup | water | 175 mL |
| ¼ cup | milk | 50 mL |
| | salt and freshly ground pepper | |
| | oil for deep frying | |
| 2 lbs | fish fillets, cut in serving pieces | 1 kg |

**Beat together** the pancake mix, water, milk, salt and pepper. (If you're drinking beer, it makes a great substitute for the milk.)

**Heat oil** in a large pot, a wok or a deep fryer over medium-high heat. Dip the fish pieces into the batter, then slide into the hot fat, 2 or 3 pieces at a time.

**Let sizzle** and pop until golden on one side. Flip over and brown the other side. The cooking time is usually less than 5 minutes. Lift from oil and drain on newspaper.

**Serve** very hot.

**Breaded fish:** Instead of dipping fish in pancake batter use breadcrumb coating as in Zucchini Fritters (page 46).

**The Chips:**

**Use 6 firm**, waxy potatoes. Peel and cut into sticks of uniform length and thickness. Place in a bowl of cold, lightly salted water for 30 minutes or so.

**Rinse and dry** potato sticks thoroughly.

**Drop them** into hot oil, a small quantity at a time, and cook over medium heat until tender but not brown. Pile partly fried chips onto a newspaper-lined platter.

**When the gang** is ready to eat, drop french fries, two handfuls at a time, back into the hot oil and cook until golden and crisp. This process only takes a few minutes.

**Serve** promptly.

**Serves 6**

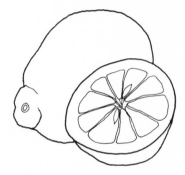

**Tip:** To test if oil is ready for deep frying. Drop in cube of bread. It should be crisp and brown with a count of 60. If it browns instantly, the oil is too hot. If the bread just sits there, the oil is not hot enough. The oil should not smoke or the food will taste terrible.

# Quick Fish Bake-Up

Particularly good with a firm sea fish.

| | | |
|---|---|---|
| 1-2 lb | fish, gutted and scaled | 1-1 kg |
| ½ tsp | salt | 2 mL |
| 2 | garlic cloves, halved | 2 |
| 3 | lemon slices | 3 |
| ¼ cup | butter | 50 mL |
| 1 tbsp | dry mustard | 15 mL |
| ½ cup | white wine | 125 mL |

**Set oven** to 450°F (230°C).

**Make three** deep slits diagonally on one side of the fish. Salt the fish well inside and out. Tuck a halved garlic clove and lemon slice into each slit.

**Cream butter** and mustard together and spread the entire fish with the mixture. Place in a greased shallow baking dish. Dribble with wine and bake, uncovered, until firm but tender, about 10 minutes per inch (2.5 cm) of thickness.

**Serve with** Lemon Potatoes (page 99) and thinly sliced tomatoes seasoned with parsley or chives.

**Serves 4**

Cook your fish with the head on to retain all the flavourful juices. The most succulent parts of the fish are the tiny morsels of flesh just under the cheeks. Try to find them.

**To test if fish is cooked:** Take the tines of a fork and place in the thick part of the flesh. Pull gently. The flesh should separate easily and be moist and light in colour. Never overcook.

# Fish Creole Style

This is particularly good with a firm sweet fish like red snapper. Excellent with pickerel, salmon or lake trout as well.

| | | |
|---|---|---|
| 1-2 lb | fish, gutted and scaled | 1-1 kg |
| 2 | limes | 2 |
| ¼ tsp | salt | 1 mL |
| ½ tsp | dried thyme | 2 mL |
| 2 | onions, chopped | 2 |
| 1 | garlic clove, chopped | 1 |
| 2 | hot chili peppers, chopped (optional) | 2 |
| 2 tbsp | oil | 25 mL |
| 3 | tomatoes, finely chopped | 3 |

**Set oven** to 450°F (230°C).

**Make three** diagonal slits on one side of the fish. Combine juice of 1 lime, salt, thyme, and half the onion, garlic and chili. Rub over whole fish and let marinate in refrigerator 1 hour.

**Heat oil** in a large frying pan. Add remaining onion, garlic and chili. Cook over medium-high heat until softened. Stir in tomatoes and let cook until well thickened.*

**Place fish** in a large greased baking dish. Spread with tomato mixture. Bake in oven 20-30 minutes, until just tender. Decorate fish with wedges of lime and sprinkle with lime juice. Serve at once.

**Serves 4**

# Fish Chowder

Fishermen have been brewing up a variation of this simple, hearty stew with their daily catch for generations.

| | | |
|---|---|---|
| 2 lbs | firm white fish fillets | 1 kg |
| 4 | bacon slices, chopped | 4 |
| 1 | medium onion, chopped | 1 |
| 1 tbsp | butter | 15 mL |
| 3 cups | potatoes, peeled and diced | 750 mL |
| 2 | carrots, chopped | 2 |
| 2 cups | boiling water | 500 mL |
| 1 | bay leaf | 1 |
| 2 cups | milk | 500 mL |
| 2 cups | table cream | 500 mL |
| | salt and freshly ground pepper | |
| 2 tbsp | fresh chopped parsley | 25 mL |
| | paprika | |
| | handful of soda crackers, roughly crumbled | |

**Cut fish** into 2″ (5 cm) pieces.

**In a large** heavy pot, sauté the bacon and onion in butter until softened. Toss in the potatoes, carrots, water and bay leaf. Cover and cook over medium heat about 10 minutes, until potatoes are tender.

**Add milk**, cream, salt and pepper. Gently stir in the fish and simmer 10 minutes.

**Ladle** into deep warm bowls and garnish with parsley, paprika and crackers. Serve with toasted Beer Break (page 178).

**Serves 6**

**Clam Chowder:** Replace fish with 2 cans (5 oz/142g each) baby clams, drained. Add water to clam juices to make the 2 cups (500 mL) liquid required to cook the vegetables.

# Scalloped Fish

How to feed a crowd with a meagre day's catch.

| | | |
|---|---|---|
| ¼ cup | butter | 50 mL |
| 2 | green onions, chopped | 2 |
| ¼ cup | flour | 50 mL |
| 2 cups | milk | 500 mL |
| 1 cup | grated Cheddar cheese | 250 mL |
| ½ tsp | salt | 2 mL |
| ¼ tsp | freshly ground pepper | 1 mL |
| ½ tsp | dry mustard | 2 mL |
| 1½ lbs | fish fillets | 750 g |
| 1 tsp | dried thyme | 5 mL |
| 1 tsp | finely chopped parsley | 5 mL |
| | paprika | |

**Set oven** to 450°F (230°C).

**Melt butter** in a medium saucepan. Add green onions and cook over medium heat until softened. Stir in the flour and cook 2 minutes.

**Remove** from heat and whisk in the milk. Return to heat. Bring to boil, stirring constantly, and cook a further 5 minutes, until sauce thickens. Stir in cheese, salt, pepper and dry mustard. Place fish fillets in a buttered baking dish. Sprinkle with thyme and parsley. Spoon sauce on top. Sprinkle with paprika.*

**Bake** approximately 20 minutes, until fish flakes when tested and the flesh is moist and juicy.

**Serves 4**

153

# Fish Burgers

This whole recipe may be done in three stages at your convenience. It's the only way to deal with a mess of boney fish.

| | | |
|---|---|---|
| 1-5 lb | fish, gutted, skinned | 1-2½ kg |
| ½ | lemon, thinly sliced | ½ |
| 1 | onion, thinly sliced | 1 |
| 2 tbsp | butter | 25 mL |
| | salt and pepper | |
| ½ cup | dry white wine | 125 mL |
| 1 recipe | Creamed Fish Sauce | 1 recipe |
| | flour | |
| 2 | eggs, beaten | 2 |
| 2 cups | dry breadcrumbs | 500 mL |
| | bacon fat, butter or oil | |

**Set oven** to 450°F (230°C).

**Rub** a large piece of foil with oil. Place the fish on top. Sprinkle with lemon, onion and bits of butter. Season, add white wine. Seal the foil.

**Place** on a baking sheet and bake for 10 minutes per inch (2.5 cm) of thickness of the fish. Flesh will be white and will flake easily. Remove from foil. Strain liquid and set aside. Lift fish flesh from bones; refrigerate until needed.

**When ready** to make into patties, add Creamed Fish Sauce to cooked, flaked fish, a little at a time, until you can form patties. (It will be fairly sticky.)

**Dip each patty** first in flour, then in a little beaten egg and finally in breadcrumbs.* Burgers may be refrigerated or frozen at this point and browned later. Brown burgers in butter.

**Serve** as is or place in hamburger buns with lots of Tartar Sauce.

**Serves 6**

## Creamed Fish Sauce

| | | |
|---|---|---|
| 2 tbsp | butter | 25 mL |
| 2 | green onions, finely chopped | 2 |
| 2 tbsp | flour | 25 mL |
| 1½ cups | hot liquid (poaching liquid from fish plus milk) | 375 mL |
| | salt and pepper | |
| 1 tsp | chopped parsley | 5 mL |

**In a small** pan, cook green onions in butter over medium heat until soft. Add the flour and cook over low heat 2 minutes.

**Remove** from heat and stir in hot liquid. Blend until smooth. Cook over medium heat 5-10 minutes, until very thick. Season with salt, pepper and parsley.

**Makes 1½ cups (375 mL)**

## Tartar Sauce

| | | |
|---|---|---|
| 1 cup | mayonnaise | 250 mL |
| 1 tbsp | sweet relish | 15 mL |
| 1 tbsp | finely chopped capers | 15 mL |
| 1 | green onion, finely chopped | 1 |
| | good squeeze lemon juice | |

**Combine** the ingredients and mix well. Best served chilled.

**Makes 1 cup (250 mL)**

**Tasty Fish Salad:** Instead of making fish burgers, combine flaked fish with mayonnaise and finely chopped green onion and celery. Season with salt and freshly ground pepper, and flavour with a good squeeze of lemon juice. Chill well before serving.

# Fish Broil

Simple seasoning to suit the catch.

| | | |
|---|---|---|
| ¼ cup | butter | 50 mL |
| 1 tbsp | finely chopped parsley | 15 mL |
| 1 tbsp | grated Parmesan cheese | 15 mL |
| ½ cup | breadcrumbs | 125 mL |
| 2 lbs | thin fish fillets | 1 kg |
| | paprika | |
| | salt and freshly ground pepper | |
| | lemon wedges | |

**Melt butter** in a small saucepan. Add the parsley, Parmesan cheese and breadcrumbs. Mix well.

**Place fish** fillets in a shallow baking dish in a single layer, spread with breadcrumb mixture and sprinkle with paprika. Slip under the broiler and cook until fish flakes easily.

**Season** with salt and pepper and serve with lemon wedges.

**Accompany** with a few asparagus spears and a Potato in Foil (page 99).

**Serves 4**

# All-Purpose Wine Sauce

A five-minute sauce that turns a simply cooked piece of fish or chicken into a taste treat.

| | | |
|---|---|---|
| 1 | tomato, peeled, seeded and chopped | 1 |
| 1-10 oz | can mushrooms, drained and sliced | 1-284 mL |
| 1 tbsp | chopped parsley | 15 mL |
| ¼ cup | butter | 50 mL |
| ½ cup | white wine | 125 mL |
| | salt and freshly ground pepper | |
| ½ cup | table cream | 125 mL |

**Sauté tomato**, mushrooms and parsley in butter in a large frying pan 5 minutes. Add wine, salt and pepper and bring to a boil. Lower heat and simmer 5 minutes.

**Add cream** and cook sauce, uncovered, until slightly thickened.

**Makes about 1 cup (250 mL)**

**Tall Tale:** It was one of those glorious summer days, hot and still, bright blue skies. Casting towards shore and trying not to latch onto one of the trees, as is often the case, a giant fish grabbed hold of the bait, leapt from the surface, then plunged to the depths. The line went taut. The wretched fish was stuck under a tree stump. A gallant friend dove into the water with mask, snorkel and net in hand, and retrieved the prize from the other side of a huge log, hook still in place. The fish didn't win any contests but it tasted great.

# Poisson au Beurre Blanc

A refined and delicate sauce for special moments. The first mouthful will instantly make up for the last minute preparation. Best made for two, or at the most, four.

| | | |
|---|---|---|
| 2 | green onions, finely chopped | 2 |
| 1 tsp | dried tarragon | 5 mL |
| ½ cup | dry white wine | 125 mL |
| 2 tbsp | white wine vinegar | 25 mL |
| 2 lbs | fish fillets (bass or trout are wonderful) | 1 kg |
| 1 cup | unsalted butter, cut in small cubes | 250 mL |

**Combine** the green onions, tarragon, white wine and vinegar in a small saucepan. Bring to a boil and cook briskly until reduced by half.

**While wine** is reducing, broil, sauté or poach the fish fillets until just cooked through.

**Off heat** whisk the butter into the flavoured wine a bit at a time. A lovely creamy sauce will start to appear. You may have to return the pan to the heat for a few moments, but be careful! If it gets too hot the butter will separate. If it does, use the sauce anyway; it will still have a marvellous flavour.

**Spoon sauce** over the fish. Serve with crisp green beans or snow peas, rice, noodles or tiny boiled potatoes.

**Serves 4**

# Fish Almondine

A classic that never wears thin.

| | | |
|---|---|---|
| 2 lbs | fish fillets | 1 kg |
| 6 tbsp | butter | 80 mL |
| 1-3 oz | package sliced almonds | 1-84 g |
| | juice of half lemon | |
| | salt and freshly ground pepper to taste | |
| | parsley or chives | |

**Set oven** to warm.

**Sauté fish** fillets in 2 tablespoons (30 mL) butter in a large skillet until flesh is flaky and opaque. Remove and set in the oven to keep warm.

**Add more** butter to the pan (about 4 tablespoons/50 mL). Toss in the almonds and stir until lightly browned.

**Squeeze in** lemon juice and pour over fish. Season with salt and pepper and sprinkle with parsley or chives.

**A crisp** green salad, sliced tomatoes and Lemon Potatoes (page 99) go very nicely.

**Serves 4**

**Simple Sauce for Fish:** Remove fish from pan when cooked. Add a little finely chopped parsley, some extra butter and a squeeze of lemon juice to the juices in the pan. Heat briefly and pour over fish.

# Stuffed Baked Fish

A particularly good dish if your catch is not quite large enough for dinner.

| | | |
|---|---|---|
| 1-2 lb | whole fish | 1 kg |
| | salt and freshly ground pepper | |
| | lemon juice | |
| 1 recipe | Savoury Stuffing for Fish | 1 recipe |
| 1 tbsp | butter | 15 mL |
| ½ cup | dry white wine (optional) | 125 mL |

**Set oven** to 450°F (230°C).

**Gut and scale** fish, leaving on head, skin and tail for better flavour.

**Sprinkle fish** cavity lightly with salt, pepper and lemon juice. Tuck in stuffing and close cavity with small skewers and string.

**Place** stuffed fish on buttered foil. Sprinkle with wine and a little more salt, pepper and lemon juice. Fold foil to enclose fish securely and place on a baking tray.

**Bake** until flesh is flaky and opaque but still moist: allow about 10 minutes per inch (2.5 cm) of thickness of stuffed fish plus 5 minutes for heat to penetrate the foil.

**Remove** baked fish to a large platter and strain delicious juices trapped in the foil into a small saucepan. Boil juices down 1-2 minutes, season to taste and swirl in a little extra butter if you like.

**Serves 4**

## Savoury Stuffing for Fish

Good for chicken and Thanksgiving turkey too.

| | | |
|---|---|---|
| ¼ cup | butter | 50 mL |
| 1 | onion, finely chopped | 1 |
| 2 cups | bread cubes, dried | 500 mL |
| 1 cup | cubed carrots | 250 mL |
| 1 cup | mushrooms, chopped | 250 mL |
| ½ cup | chopped fresh parsley | 125 mL |
| 2 tsp | lime juice or lemon juice | 10 mL |
| 1 | egg | 1 |
| 1 | garlic clove, minced | 1 |
| 2 tsp | salt | 10 mL |
| ¼ tsp | freshly ground pepper | 1 mL |
| ¼ tsp | dried marjoram | 1 mL |

**Melt butter** in a heavy frying pan. Add onion and cook gently over medium heat until softened.

**Toss** buttery onion with remaining ingredients and stuff lightly into fish cavity.

**Makes 3 cups (750 mL)**

**Record the catch:** Draw around your fish with a black marker on newspaper. Write on it the name of the fisherman, the date, the time of day, the weather conditions and the successful lure.

# Tuna Spread

A light summery sauce. Good on hard-boiled eggs and thin slices of cooked cold chicken, pork or veal.

| | | |
|---|---|---|
| 1-6½ oz | can solid white tuna | 1-185 g |
| 2 tbsp | lemon juice | 25 mL |
| 2 tbsp | olive oil | 25 mL |
| ½ cup | mayonnaise | 125 mL |
| ¼ cup | olives, pitted and chopped | 50 mL |
| 1 tbsp | capers | 15 mL |

**Drain** and flake tuna.

**Combine** lemon juice, oil and mayonnaise in a blender jar. Gradually add tuna, olives and capers and blend until smooth.

**Cover** and chill.

**Makes 1 cup (250 mL)**

# Smoked Fish Pâté

Smoked trout, or any smoked fish, makes a wonderful snack.

| | | |
|---|---|---|
| ½ lb | smoked fish | 250 g |
| 2 | green onions, finely chopped | 2 |
| 1 tsp | finely chopped parsley | 5 mL |
| 1 tsp | prepared horseradish | 5 mL |
| 1 tbsp | lemon juice | 15 mL |
| ¼ cup | mayonnaise | 50 mL |

**Remove** all bones from fish and separate into flakes.

**Blend** or mash all ingredients together to make a smooth spread. Pack into a small bowl, cover and chill.*

**Serve with** crisp wholewheat toast or crisp bread.

**Makes 1 cup (250 mL)**

# Fish Bobcaygeon Style

The fishing guides on the Trent River used to keep huge oil cans of bacon fat in the bows of their boats. The morning's catch, usually bass or pickerel, was cooked up fresh every noon on shore. Here's their method. Unusual and superb.

| | bacon fat | |
|---|---|---|
| ½ lb | bacon | 250 g |
| 2 lbs | fish fillets, well dried | 1 kg |

**Half fill** a large, deep frying pan with bacon fat and heat until almost smoking. (Do be careful of fire.) Drop in the bacon. In moments it will be crisp. Remove and set on paper towels to drain.

**Slip fish** fillets into the hot fat 2 or 3 minutes. Remove and drain. Eat bacon and fish immediately.

**Serves 4**

## Campfire Trout

Best eaten as the sun comes up. Cook 2 or 3 slices bacon until crisp in a heavy frying pan. Remove from pan and set aside. Dip small trout in flour or cornmeal and fry in bacon fat until fish flakes and skin is golden. Serve at once with steaming cups of campfire coffee.

## Campfire Coffee

Measure cups of water into a pan and bring to the boil. Toss in 1 tablespoon (15 mL) ground coffee per cup (250 mL) plus 1 for the pot, with a tiny pinch of salt. Bring whole lot just to boiling point, then lift pan from heat. Stir and let rest 3 or 4 minutes. Strain into mugs. Sip as you watch the sun rise.

# From the Sea

**To boil a lobster:** Fill a large pot with water, add 1 tablespoon (15 mL) salt and bring to a rolling boil. Grab live lobster on the back just behind the head and plunge it head first into boiling water. Lower heat, cover pot and simmer about 5 minutes for the first pound (450 g) and 3 minutes for each additional pound. (For example, a 2-pounder (1 kg) will be ready in 8 minutes.) Split lobster in half from end to end, remove stomach and intestines, just behind the head. Dip morsels of lobster meat in melted butter spiked with lemon juice and have a feast.

**Simple steamed clams:** Scrub fresh clams to remove sand. Place them in a large pot with 3 finely chopped green onions, 1 tablespoon (15 mL) butter, a few sprigs of parsley, a pinch of thyme and 1 cup (250 mL) dry white wine. Cover pot tightly and cook over medium heat until clams open. (Throw away those that do not open within 15 minutes.) Lift clams from pot. Ladle into warm bowls and garnish with a sprinkling of chopped parsley.

**Steamed mussels:** First, clean the mussels carefully before cooking or you will have mouthfuls of grit. Scrub them well; tug the hairy strands attached to the shells and cut away. Soak mussels in cold water a couple of hours. Drain, rinse in fresh water and prepare as for steamed clams, above.

# Partridge Paella

What do you do with one sorry-looking partridge, brought home by the triumphant once-a-year hunter. You might be inclined to throw it out but we've finally found the solution. Partridge Paella.

| | | |
|---|---|---|
| 4 tbsp | oil | 60 mL |
| 1 | onion, chopped | 1 |
| 1 | garlic clove, chopped | 1 |
| 1 | green pepper, chopped | 1 |
| 1½ cups | rice | 375 mL |
| 1 tsp | turmeric | 5 mL |
| 1-14 oz | can tomatoes | 1-398 mL |
| 1-5 oz | can clams, plus liquid | 1-142 g |
| 2 cups | chicken stock | 500 mL |
| 1 or 2 | partridge, cleaned | 1 or 2 |
| | bay leaf | |
| | salt and freshly ground pepper to taste | |
| 1-4 oz | can shrimp, drained | 1-113 g |

**Heat** 2 tablespoons (30 mL) oil in a large frying pan and cook the onion, garlic, green pepper and rice over medium-high heat until the rice is a light nutty colour. Stir in the turmeric. Drain the tomatoes (reserving juice), chop roughly and add to the rice.

**Combine** the tomato juice, clam liquid and enough chicken stock to make 3 cups (750 mL). Pour over rice. Add bay leaf, salt and pepper.

**Cut** partridge in half and, in another pan, brown lightly in remaining oil. Tuck into the rice.

**Bring** to a boil. Lower heat and cover until rice is plump and the juices have been absorbed, about 30 minutes.* Stir in the clams and shrimp for last 10 minutes of cooking.

**Garnish** with lemon wedges and serve with Herb-Garlic Bread (page 53).

**Serves 6**

# Game Casserole

Argh! Deer and moose season is upon us again. What to do with pounds of unrecognizable cuts of meat, frozen and wrapped up in unmarked brown paper? Any cut will be delicious if cooked properly.

| | | |
|---|---|---|
| 2 lbs | venison or moose meat | 1 kg |
| ½ cup | flour, seasoned with salt and freshly ground pepper | 125 mL |
| 4 | eggs, beaten with 2 tbsp (25 mL) table cream | 4 |
| ½ cup | breadcrumbs | 125 mL |
| 1 tbsp | chopped fresh parsley | 15 mL |
| ¼ cup | grated Parmesan cheese | 50 mL |
| | butter | |
| ½ cup | port (red wine doesn't have the body, Madeira is too strong) | 125 mL |

**Set oven** to 350°F (180°C).

**Cut meat** into 1½″ (4 cm) cubes. Flatten to ¼″ (6 mm) thickness, using a mallet. Shake pieces in flour. Dip in beaten egg and toss in a mixture of breadcrumbs, parsley and grated Parmesan cheese to coat well.*

**Sauté** breaded meat in butter until lightly browned. Place in a baking dish and pour in port. Cook, covered, in oven until tender, about 1½ hours.

**Serves 4**

# Roast Wild Duck

With any luck your friendly hunter will have the foresight to clean his ducks before he brings them over.

| | | |
|---|---|---|
| 2 | wild ducks, cleaned | 2 |
| 1 | apple, peeled, cored and quartered | 1 |
| 1 | onion, halved | 1 |
| 2 | cinnamon sticks | 2 |
| 4 | bacon slices | 4 |
| ½ cup | port | 125 mL |

**Set oven** to 400°F (200°C).

**Tuck** apple, onion and cinnamon sticks into the duck cavities. Truss ducks and place in roasting pan.

**Drape with** bacon slices. Roast approximately 1-1½ hours. Remove ducks from pan.

**Add port** to the roasting pan and boil over high heat, stirring constantly. Serve with ducks.

**Serves 4**

# Loafing Around

**W**hen it rains steadily for the second day in a row, the mood in camp is often oppressively gloomy. You find yourself with a houseful of irritable people underfoot with nothing to do. Set them to baking (with this handy text at hand) while you settle down in the most comfortable spot with a good novel.

Good humour is soon restored with the anticipation of hot, chewy, fudgy caramel bars or the irresistible aroma of brownies fresh from the oven.

Here is a selection of sweet snacking food: some of it sturdy enough to give sustenance on summer and winter hikes and some of it for those times when you just fancy a little treat. Here, too, are a few alternatives for times when the breadbox is empty and the local store offers only flannel bread.

# Lemon Wafers

Resolve that you will have good bread, and never cease striving after this result till you have effected it. If persons without brains can accomplish this, why cannot you?

*Housekeeping in Old Virginia*

A light sugar cookie. Delicious with fresh fruit or ice cream desserts.

| | | |
|---|---|---|
| 1 cup | butter, softened | 250 mL |
| 1 cup | sugar | 250 mL |
| 1 | egg | 1 |
| 2¼ cups | all-purpose flour | 550 mL |
| ½ tsp | baking soda | 2 mL |
| | pinch salt | |
| 1 tsp | grated lemon rind | 5 mL |
| | sliced almonds (optional) | |

**Set oven** to 400°F (200°C).

**Cream butter** with sugar until light and fluffy, then beat in egg.

**Sift together flour**, baking soda and salt and add to the creamed ingredients with the lemon rind.

**Stir** until thoroughly mixed.

**Form dough** into two rolls, about 1½" (4 cm) in diameter. Wrap well and set in the refrigerator 1 hour or until needed.

**Slice roll** into rounds about ¼" (5 mm) thick and place on lightly greased baking sheets. Set a sliced almond on top of each one, if you like.

**Bake** 7-8 minutes, until cookies are just beginning to colour. Remove from sheets and cool on wire racks.

**Makes 6 dozen wafers**

**Chocolate Wafers:** Proceed as for Lemon Wafers but use 2 cups (500 mL) flour, ¼ cup (50 mL) cocoa and a pinch of cinnamon instead of the 2¼ cups (550 mL) flour. Omit lemon rind.

# Midnight Munchies

These are delicious, crisp, buttery cookies. They're quick and simple to make.

| | | |
|---|---|---|
| ¾ cup | butter | 175 mL |
| ½ cup | brown sugar | 125 mL |
| 1 cup | all-purpose flour | 250 mL |
| 1 cup | rolled oats | 250 mL |
| ½ tsp | baking powder | 2 mL |
| ½ tsp | baking soda | 2 mL |
| ½ tsp | salt | 2 mL |

**Set oven** to 350°F (180°C).

**Cream together** butter and sugar. Toss the other ingredients together and combine well with creamed butter.

**Drop** by spoonfuls onto lightly greased cookie sheets and press with tines of a lightly floured fork to flatten.

**Bake** in oven until golden brown, 10-15 minutes. Set on wire racks to cool.

**Makes 24**

**Date and Oatmeal Cookie:** Combine 1 cup (250 mL) pitted and halved dates with 2 tablespoons (25 mL) lemon juice in a small pan. Add water to cover. Simmer over medium heat, stirring constantly, until thick and smooth. Cool mixture and sandwich a tablespoon (15 mL) of this tasty date filling between two cookies.

# Granola Bars

A sustaining snack to take along on rigorous hikes.

| | | |
|---|---|---|
| ¾ cup | all-purpose flour | 175 mL |
| ½ tsp | baking soda | 2 mL |
| ½ tsp | salt | 2 mL |
| 1 tsp | cinnamon | 5 mL |
| ½ cup | butter | 125 mL |
| ¾ cup | brown sugar | 175 mL |
| 1 | egg | 1 |
| 1 tsp | vanilla | 5 mL |
| 2½ cups | Granola (page 41) | 625 mL |
| ½ cup | raisins or chocolate chips | 125 mL |

**Set oven** to 375°F (190°C).

**Sift together flour**, soda, salt and cinnamon.

**Cream butter** with sugar until light and fluffy.

**Add egg** and vanilla.

**Stir in** flour mixture and gently fold in granola and raisins or other goodies.

**Turn into** a lightly greased 8" x 8" (2 L) pan and bake 15-20 minutes, until a toothpick inserted near centre comes out clean. Cut into bars when cool.

**Makes 16 2-inch (5 cm) bars**

**Good for the trail:** Mixtures of dried fruit, nuts and seeds make good wholesome snacking food. Try combining equal quantities of peanuts, raisins and hulled sunflower seeds. Or, for a change of taste, add a few cashews, chocolate chips or unsweetened coconut slivers.

# Chocolate Chews

Sinfully rich and fudgy. These brownies keep well in a sealed container if not immediately devoured.

| | | |
|---|---|---|
| 3-1 oz | squares unsweetened chocolate | 3-28 g |
| ½ cup | butter | 125 mL |
| 3 | eggs | 3 |
| ½ tsp | salt | 2 mL |
| 1 tsp | vanilla | 5 mL |
| 1½ cups | sugar | 375 mL |
| 1 cup | all-purpose flour | 250 mL |
| ½ cup | chopped walnuts | 125 mL |

**Set oven** to 350°F (180°C).

**Melt chocolate** and butter in the top of a double boiler, over simmering water. Set aside to cool slightly.

**Beat eggs** with salt and vanilla, gradually add the sugar and beat until smooth. Add the cooled chocolate. Blend well. Add the flour and walnuts and stir until well mixed.

**Spoon** into a lightly greased 9″ x 13″ (3L) baking pan. Bake 25-30 minutes. Cool before cutting.

**Makes 24 2-inch (5 cm) squares**

# Chewy Caramel Bars

A warning! Be prepared to make these several times once you've tried them.

| | | |
|---|---|---|
| 1 cup | all-purpose flour | 250 mL |
| ½ cup | butter | 125 mL |
| 3 tbsp | white sugar | 45 mL |
| 2 | eggs, beaten | 2 |
| 2 tbsp | all-purpose flour | 25 mL |
| 1 cup | chopped walnuts | 250 mL |
| 1½ cups | brown sugar | 375 mL |
| ½ cup | unsweetened desiccated coconut | 125 mL |
| ½ tsp | vanilla | 2 mL |

**Set oven** to 350°F (180°C).

**Cream together** the flour, butter and sugar. Press mixture into a lightly greased 8" x 8" (2 L) pan and bake 10-15 minutes.

**Toss together** the remaining ingredients. Spoon onto baked layer. Return to oven and continue baking 25-30 minutes.

**Cool** and cut into squares.

**Makes 16 2-inch (5 cm) squares**

**Tip:** To keep a round-bottomed bowl from slipping, place on a wet tea towel, folded in three.

# Giant Chocolate Chip Cookies

The Cookie Monster variety.

| | | |
|---|---|---|
| 1 cup | butter | 250 mL |
| 1½ cups | firmly packed brown sugar | 375 mL |
| 2 | eggs, well beaten | 2 |
| 1 tsp | vanilla | 5 mL |
| 1½ cups | all-purpose flour | 375 mL |
| 1 tsp | baking soda | 5 mL |
| ½ tsp | salt | 2 mL |
| ½ tsp | cinnamon | 2 mL |
| 2½ cups | rolled oats | 625 mL |
| 1 cup | chocolate chips | 250 mL |

**Set oven** to 375°F (190°C).

**Cream butter** until fluffy. Add sugar and blend well.

**Beat in** the eggs and vanilla.

**Sift together** the flour, soda, salt and cinnamon and add to the creamed mixture. Stir in oats and chocolate chips.

**Using** a ⅓ cup (50 mL) measure, drop the batter onto lightly greased baking sheets. With a greased fork, flatten each cookie into a circle, approximately 4 inches (10 cm) in diameter.

**Bake** 12-15 minutes, until firm to the touch and nicely browned.

**Set on** wire racks to cool.

**Makes 18 giant cookies**

These make great little cookies too.

# Spicy Carrot Cake

A good moist snacking cake.

| | | |
|---|---|---|
| 2½ cups all-purpose flour | | 375 mL |
| 2 tsp | baking soda | 10 mL |
| 1 tsp | cinnamon | 5 mL |
| 1 tsp | salt | 5 mL |
| 1 cup | oil | 250 mL |
| 2 cups | sugar | 500 mL |
| 4 | eggs | 4 |
| 1 tsp | vanilla | 5 mL |
| 3 cups | grated carrot | 750 mL |
| 1 cup | chopped walnuts | 250 mL |

**Set oven** to 350°F (180°C).

**Grease** 9" x 13" (3 L) baking pan and dust with flour.

**Sift together** flour, baking soda, cinnamon and salt.

**Combine** oil, sugar, eggs and vanilla in another large bowl and beat until light with an electric mixer or a whisk.

**Stir in** grated carrot. Swiftly blend in dry ingredients, one-third at a time. Add nuts.

**Pour batter** into prepared pan and bake about 40-45 minutes or until cake is cooked through.

**Let cake stand** in pan 10 minutes, then turn out onto a rack and cool completely. Ice with Cream Cheese Frosting.

## Cream Cheese Frosting

| 1-4 oz | package cream cheese | 1-125 g |
|---|---|---|
| ½ cup | butter | 125 mL |
| 2 cups | icing sugar | 500 mL |
| 1 tbsp | lemon juice | 15 mL |

**Cream cheese** and butter. Beat in sugar and lemon juice.

**Zucchini cake:** Replace grated carrot with 3 cups (750 mL) grated zucchini and include ½ teaspoon (2 mL) grated nutmeg.

**Apple cake:** Substitute grated apple for grated carrot and add ¼ teaspoon (1 mL) ground cloves.

**Non-stick cake pans:** It's frustrating to turn out a cake only to find that half of it has stuck in the pan. Rub the inside of the pan with *unsalted* fat (butter or shortening) and toss in a little flour. Tip pan around to cover inside of pan completely with flour, turn upside down and tap it to remove any excess.

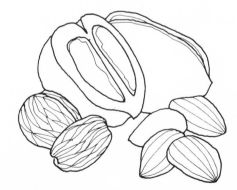

# Beer Break

This bread takes roughly three minutes to put together before it's popped in the oven. Wonderful for soup dunking or mopping up juices (fresh toasted and drenched in butter). The secret is in the self-raising flour—which contains the magic to make the bread rise.

| | | |
|---|---|---|
| 3 cups | self-raising flour | 750 mL |
| 3 tbsp | sugar | 45 mL |
| 1-12 oz | bottle beer | 1-341 mL |
| 1 cup | grated Cheddar cheese | 250 mL |

**Set oven** to 350°F (180°C).

**Combine** flour and sugar in a large bowl. Gradually stir in beer and cheese.

**Turn batter** into a greased 9" x 5" (2 L) loaf pan and bake 45-50 minutes.

**Cool** on a wire rack.

# Never-fail Birthday Cake

It's almost certain that one young visitor or family member will have a birthday over the holidays. Here is a never-fail cake for the least ambitious cook. Have in the store cupboard a lemon cake mix. One that calls for oil and 3-4 eggs will make a rich, moist cake. Combine ingredients and bake, following instructions on the cake package. A ring baking pan is especially effective and then any available candle can be stuck in the middle. Glaze with a simple frosting of lemon juice and icing sugar and decorate with lots of Smarties.

# Kettle Loaf

Five-minute preparation, forty minutes in the oven. If you have an old-fashioned cast iron Dutch oven, bake the bread in that. Grease it well. Slip the dough in. Cover and bake. It's wonderful. That's how bread used to be baked over a peat fire.

| | | |
|---|---|---|
| 7 cups | all-purpose flour | 1.75 L |
| 2 tsp | salt | 10 mL |
| ½ tsp | baking soda | 2 mL |
| 2 tbsp | baking powder | 25 mL |
| ½ cup | raisins | 125 mL |
| ½ cup | caraway seeds (optional) | 125 mL |
| 2 tbsp | honey | 25 mL |
| 4 cups | buttermilk | 1 L |

**Set oven** to 350°F (180°C).

**Toss together** dry ingredients in a bowl. Stir in the raisins and caraway seeds.

**Gradually add** the honey and buttermilk. Get right in there with your hands to mix. It's fun.

**Turn onto** a floured board. Shape the dough into 2 rounded loaves (it's very sticky but that's what makes it fun!). Place on a baking tray.

**Make** a deep cross in each one with a sharp knife. Bake 40 minutes, then cool on a wire rack.

**Serve with** bowls of butter and a Little Pot o' Jam (page 39).

**Makes 2 loaves**

If you stumble across a bag of stone ground wholewheat flour, use that. Divine!

# Country Muffins

An old-fashioned wholesome muffin. This batter, without the apple, raisins and orange rind, keeps well, covered in the refrigerator, for up to 2 weeks.

| | | |
|---|---|---|
| 3 cups | bran flakes | 750 mL |
| 1 cup | boiling water | 250 mL |
| 2½ cups | all-purpose flour | 625 mL |
| ¼ cup | brown sugar | 50 mL |
| ½ tsp | salt | 2 mL |
| 2½ tsp | baking soda | 15 mL |
| 1 tsp | cinnamon | 5 mL |
| 1 tsp | allspice | 5 mL |
| 2 | eggs, beaten | 2 |
| 1¾ cups | buttermilk | 425 mL |
| ½ cup | vegetable oil | 125 mL |
| ½ cup | molasses | 125 mL |
| ½ cup | grated apple | 125 mL |
| 1 cup | raisins | 250 mL |
| 2 tsp | grated orange rind | 10 mL |

**Set oven** to 400°F (200°C).

**Grease** 18 muffin cups. In a large bowl, combine the bran flakes and boiling water. Stir and set aside to cool.

**Sift together** dry ingredients.

**Add eggs**, buttermilk, oil and molasses to cooled, moist bran. With a few swift strokes, fold in the sifted dry ingredients.* When partially mixed, add the apple, raisins and orange rind.

**Fill** muffin cups just to the top, using a ⅓ cup (50 mL) measure. Bake approximately 20 minutes.

**Makes 18 giant muffins**

**Tip:** When a recipe includes oil and molasses, honey or corn syrup, measure the oil first. The others then slip out of the measuring cup without sticking.

# Cornmeal Muffins

A nutty-flavoured muffin, equally good sweet or savoury.

| | | |
|---|---|---|
| 1 cup | all-purpose flour | 250 mL |
| 1 cup | yellow cornmeal | 250 mL |
| 2 tsp | baking powder | 10 mL |
| ½ tsp | salt | 2 mL |
| ¼ cup | sugar | 50 mL |
| 1 | egg, beaten | 1 |
| 1 cup | milk | 250 mL |
| ¼ cup | melted butter or shortening | 50 mL |

**Set oven** to 425°F (220°C).
*375°*
**Grease** 12 muffin cups.

**Toss together** dry ingredients in a large bowl.

**Combine egg** and milk and blend quickly into dry ingredients. Stir in melted butter or shortening.

**Spoon** about ⅓ cup (75 mL) batter into each muffin cup, filling cups ¾ full.

**Bake** 15-20 minutes.

**Makes 12 muffins**

**Cornmeal Cheese Muffins:** Add ½ cup (125 mL) grated nippy Cheddar cheese to the cornmeal batter.
**Cornmeal Muffin Surprise:** Spoon batter into muffin cups, filling each ⅓ full. Add 1 teaspoon (5 mL) marmalade or apricot jam and fill cups ¾ full with remaining batter.
**Blueberry Corn Muffins:** Add 1 cup (250 mL) blueberries to cornmeal batter.

# Fool Proof Pastry

In spite of the myths about handling pastry with kid gloves, this traditional mix seems to withstand all kinds of punishment and still ends up light and flaky.

| 5 cups | all-purpose flour | 1.25 L |
|--------|-------------------|--------|
| 1 tsp | salt | 5 mL |
| 1 lb | lard, chilled | 500 g |
| 1 | egg | 1 |
| 1 tbsp | lemon juice or vinegar | 15 mL |
| | cold water | |

**Mix flour** and salt in a large bowl.

**Cut in** the lard, using two knives or a pastry blender, until mixture resembles coarse crumbs.

**Break egg** into a 1 cup (250 mL) measure. Add lemon juice or vinegar and enough ice-cold water to fill the cup (250 mL).

**Stir liquid** into flour mix (add only enough so that the dough may be gathered together to make a ball). Knead briefly and divide into 2 balls. Wrap securely and chill 30 minutes before rolling out.

**This pastry** dough can be stored in the refrigerator for a few days or frozen for up to 3 weeks.

**Makes 2 9-inch (23 cm) double-crust pies**

**Pastry Tip:** Partially bake the pastry crust for your quiche or fruit tart if you like it to be crisp rather than soft. Place pastry in pie plate in usual way and prick several times with a fork. Press a piece of buttered foil against the inside of pastry shell and fill with dried beans. Bake at 400°F (200°C) 8 minutes. Remove beans and foil and return pie shell to the oven 3-4 minutes. For a fully baked pie shell continue the baking a further 5 minutes.

# Basic Pizza Crust

This crust is extra quick and easy: five minutes to mix and forty-five minutes to rise.

| | | |
|---|---|---|
| 2-2½ cups | all-purpose flour | 500-625 mL |
| 2 tsp | sugar | 10 mL |
| 1 tsp | salt | 5 mL |
| 1 tbsp | fast-acting active dry yeast | 15 mL |
| 1 cup | hot water | 250 mL |
| ¼ cup | olive oil | 50 mL |

**Mix** 1 cup flour with the sugar, salt and yeast in a large bowl.

**Combine** hot water and oil. Add to dry ingredients and beat diligently until smooth.

**Gradually** stir in more flour to make a soft dough.

**Turn out** onto a floured counter and knead 4-5 minutes.

**Form dough** into a ball, place in a greased bowl and turn so top of dough is greased.

**Cover** and let stand in a warm place until doubled in size, about 45 minutes.

**Punch down**. Proceed as for Pizza (page 83) or store for future use.

**Makes 2 12-inch (30 cm) pizzas or 1 large rectangular pizza**

**Pizza dough on hand:** Press pizza dough onto pizza tins or baking sheets, wrap securely and freeze, or freeze in the ball. For a thin, crisp pizza crust, press dough onto tins and prebake in a 400°F (200°C) oven 10 minutes. Cool, wrap and freeze. For a deeper, softer crust allow dough to rest 10 minutes at room temperature on the tins before prebaking.

**Fast-rising yeast dough:** Place a large shallow pan on the bottom rack of a cold oven and pour in boiling water to a depth of 1" (2.5cm). Set dough to rise in a cloth-covered bowl set on a rack above the pan.

# Banana Bread

When baking with bananas, the riper they are the more intense the flavour and the better the taste. So be glad when you find two or three overripe bananas forgotten in the fruit bowl.

| | | |
|---|---|---|
| 2 cups | all-purpose flour | 500 mL |
| ½ tsp | salt | 2 mL |
| 1 tsp | baking soda | 5 mL |
| ½ cup | butter | 125 mL |
| 1 cup | sugar | 250 mL |
| 2 | eggs | 2 |
| 2 | ripe bananas, mashed | 2 |
| ⅓ cup | sour cream | 75 mL |
| ½ cup | chopped walnuts | 125 mL |

**Set oven** to 350°F (180°C).

**Grease** and flour 9" x 5" (2 L) loaf pan.

**Sift together** dry ingredients.

**Beat butter** with sugar in a large bowl until mixture is light and creamy. Beat in eggs.

**Add** mashed bananas. Stir in flour mixture alternately with the sour cream and then fold in nuts.

**Pour batter** into prepared pan and bake about 1 hour. Leave in pan 10 minutes before turning out onto a rack to cool.

**Keeps well** if wrapped in foil and may be frozen.

# Super Bread

| 2 | eggs, beaten | 2 |
|---|---|---|
| 2 tbsp | shortening, melted | 25 mL |
| | oil | |

In roughly fifteen minutes you can have a mound of soft bread dough that can be shoved in your fridge. At your leisure, just grab a hunk of dough, plop it in a pan, let it rise and pop it in the oven.

The dough will keep, covered with plastic wrap, in the refrigerator for one week, to be used at will. With this simple recipe you can make pizzas, sticky buns, big buns, little buns, cheese bread, plain bread, pepperoni bread. It's fun, it's quick and it's foolproof.

| 2 tbsp (2 pkgs) | fast-rising active dry yeast | 25 mL |
|---|---|---|
| ½ cup | sugar | 125 mL |
| 2½ cups | warm water | 625 mL |
| 8 cups | all-purpose flour (you may use a little more or a little less) | 2 kg |
| 1 tbsp | salt | 15 mL |

**Combine yeast**, sugar and ½ cup (125 mL) water in a large warm bowl.

**Sift together** the flour and salt.

**When yeast** has started to bubble, after about 5 minutes, add the eggs and shortening. Gradually beat in the flour alternately with the remaining water until the mixture forms a rough and sticky ball.

**Turn out** onto a floured board. The rule books will tell you to knead 15 minutes. If you're feeling aggressive, go ahead; if you're in a hurry, 3 or 4 minutes will suffice as long as the dough becomes smooth and not sticky.

**Lightly brush** the dough all over with oil. Place in a greased bowl. Cover with plastic wrap and refrigerate until ready to use. Punch dough down daily.

**Before using** dough from the refrigerator make sure it has had a chance to rise once (usually 3-4 hours). After that you can use it whenever you wish.

**If you wish** to use the dough immediately, set in a warm place and let rise about 1 hour, until nice and plump (double in size). Punch dough down and use in any of the following recipes. If using dough direct from refrigerator, punch down first. Remember dough from the refrigerator will take longer to rise. Prepare the recipe, stick it in a corner and forget about it for a couple of hours. You can prepare any of the recipes and let them rise in the refrigerator overnight. Make sure to grease the tops well. The outside will be very crunchy when baked.

**Kneading:** Push the centre of the dough away from you with the heel of your hand, then pull the edge towards you. Give the dough a quarter turn and repeat. There's nothing to it.

## Homemade Bread

If you wish to make only one loaf of bread, use half the dough.

| 1 recipe | Super Bread | 1 recipe |
|---|---|---|
|  | melted butter or 1 egg white, beaten with a little water |  |

**Set oven** to 375°F (190°C).

**Knead and shape** dough into a ball.

**Pat or roll** dough into a rectangle on a lightly floured board.

**Fold in** thirds lengthwise and pinch ends to seal. Place the dough in a greased 9" x 5" (2L) loaf pan, seam side down. Cover with a tea towel and let rise in a warm corner until nice and plump (double in size), about 1-2 hours.

**Brush top** with melted butter or a little egg white beaten with water to make a crisp golden crust.

**Bake** 40-45 minutes or until loaf is lightly browned and edges have come slightly away from pan. Turn out onto a rack and just try to resist the temptation to cut before cooling.

**Cheese and Pepperoni Loaf:** Proceed as for Homemade Bread. After shaping dough into a rectangle spread with 2 tablespoons (25 mL) softened butter. Sprinkle liberally with grated Cheddar cheese and chopped pepperoni. Sprinkle with paprika. Continue following method for Homemade Bread.

## Sticky Buns

The all-time favourite. One third of the dough will make a dozen rolls.

| 1 recipe | Super Bread | 1 recipe |
|---|---|---|
| 4 tbsp | softened butter | 50 mL |
| 2 tbsp +½ cup | brown sugar | 25 mL +125 mL |
| 1 tsp | ground cinnamon | 5 mL |
| ½ cup | raisins | 125 mL |

**Set oven** to 350°F (180°C).

**Knead dough** and shape into a ball.

**Pat or roll** into a rectangle on a lightly floured board. Spread dough with 2 tablespoons (25 mL) softened butter.

**Sprinkle** with 2 tablespoons (25 mL) brown sugar and the ground cinnamon and raisins. Roll up the dough length-wise and cut in 1½" (4 cm) widths.

**Melt** 2 tablespoons (25 mL) butter in a small saucepan with ½ cup (125 mL) brown sugar. Spread on the bottom of a lightly buttered large glass pie plate or square pan.

**Place rolls** in pan, cut edge down. Cover with a tea towel and let rise in a warm corner until nice and plump (double in size), about 1-2 hours.

**Bake** 35-40 minutes, until lightly browned.

## Buns

One quarter of the dough will make a dozen dinner rolls. Work with one quarter of the dough at a time.

| 1 recipe | Super Bread | 1 recipe |
|---|---|---|
|  | melted butter |  |

**Set oven** to 375°F (190°C).

**Knead dough** and shape into a ball.

**Roll** into a cylinder shape. Divide dough into 12. Shape each piece into a small ball. Arrange in a lightly buttered glass pie plate or square pan. Cover with a tea towel and let rise in a warm corner until nice and plump (double in size), about 1-2 hours.

**Brush tops** with melted butter. Bake 20 minutes, until lightly browned.

# Sweet Things

For us the sweetest treat in the whole world is a bowl of freshly picked wild blueberries with thick, rich cream poured over. We sneak off to a solitary rock and savour them one by one. There are few more delicious desserts than fresh ripe fruit, perhaps tossed in a little sugar with a dash of liqueur. Sometimes, however, when you've just finished a good book and you have a relaxed half hour, you *may* feel like having some fun in the kitchen.

Home-made desserts are a rare treat: everyone from toddler to grandparent loves fruit crisp hot from the oven with softly whipped cream or fresh fruit parfait.

All of these sweet things can be whipped together within half an hour. They look and taste wonderful, but the cook does not need a 'Cordon Bleu' diploma to make them.

# Bananas from the Sun

# Scotch Parfait

Euery thing hath an end, and a pudding hath two.
*Four letters confuted (1592), Thomas Nashe*

Simplicity at its best. Serve hot or cold with large spoonfuls of whipped cream.

| 4 | bananas | 4 |
|---|---|---|
| 2 tbsp | sugar | 25 mL |
| 2 tbsp | lemon juice | 25 mL |
| 2 tbsp | dark rum | 25 mL |
| 2 tbsp | butter | 25 mL |

**Peel bananas** and cut in half lengthwise. Sprinkle with sugar, lemon juice and rum and let stand 30 minutes, turning occasionally.

**Melt butter** in a frying pan. Add bananas and their sweet juices. Shaking the pan gently, cook bananas over medium-low heat until heated through.

**Serves 4**

For something a little more spectacular, add a little extra rum to the bananas and light.

Not quite the same as on the rocks. Great spooned on hot coffee if you can't wait for it to chill.

| ¾ cup | liquid honey | 175 mL |
|---|---|---|
| ½ cup | Scotch whisky | 125 mL |
| 1 tbsp | lemon juice | 15 mL |
| 2 cups | whipping cream | 500 mL |

**Blend together** honey, Scotch and lemon juice in a bowl.

**Gradually beat** in the whipping cream and beat until firm but not stiff. Pour into wine glasses and refrigerate until set.

**Serves 4**

For a special treat fold in toasted ground almonds.

# Strawberry Decadence

Light, luscious and quite sinful: a dessert that may be adapted for other tender fruits.

| | | |
|---|---|---|
| 1 quart | strawberries | 1 L |
| 1 tsp | fruit sugar | 5 mL |
| 1 tbsp | lemon juice | 15 mL |
| 2 tbsp | kirsch or orange liqueur | 25 mL |
| 1 cup | whipping cream | 250 mL |
| 1 pint | ice cream | 500 mL |
| 1 tbsp | liqueur (same as above) | 15 mL |

**Wash strawberries** and cut in half. Reserve a few whole strawberries for garnish and marinate the others in mixture of sugar, lemon juice and 2 tablespoons (25 mL) kirsch.

**Beat whipping** cream until stiff but not dry. Beat the ice cream with a whisk until smooth but not melted.

**Combine** the whipping cream with the ice cream and 1 tablespoon (15 mL) liqueur. Fold in strawberries and serve in glass bowls.

**Garnish with** whole strawberries.

**Serves 6**

# Super Sundae

Serve scoops of ice cream with the following sauces and fruits and nuts to go on top.

## Strawberry Sundae Sauce

This pure, fresh fruit sauce is also delicious with pancakes and crêpes.

| | | |
|---|---|---|
| 1 pint | strawberries | 500 mL |
| 1 tbsp | orange liqueur | 15 mL |
| 1 tbsp | lemon juice | 15 mL |
| 1 tbsp | sugar | 15 mL |

**Wash and slice** strawberries. Sprinkle with orange liqueur, lemon juice and sugar. Let stand one hour. Blend.

**Makes 1 cup (250 mL)**

## Chocolate Sauce

Rich and very chocolatey. Particularly good when served warm over frozen desserts. Add orange liqueur for a special treat.

| | | |
|---|---|---|
| 4-1 oz | squares unsweetened chocolate | 4-28 g |
| 1 cup | sugar | 250 mL |
| ⅔ cup | table cream | 150 mL |
| | pinch salt | |
| 1 tsp | vanilla | 5 mL |
| 2 tbsp | butter | 25 mL |

**Melt chocolate** with sugar, cream and salt in a bowl set over a pan of simmering water. Stir until completely smooth. Remove from heat and add vanilla and butter.

**Makes 1 cup (250 mL)**

**Chocolate Substitute:** In most instances you may substitute 3 tablespoons (45 mL) cocoa plus 1 tablespoon (15 mL) butter for each square (1 oz/28g) unsweetened chocolate.

# Tropical Fruit Cooler

A huge bowl of fruit lightly flavoured with liqueurs is always spectacular to serve during the summer months. It travels well too.

| | | |
|---|---|---|
| 2 | melons (1 honeydew, 1 canteloupe) | 2 |
| 1 | fresh pineapple | 1 |
| 1 pint | fresh strawberries, cut in half | 500 mL |
| 1 | tart apple, peeled, cored and sliced | 1 |
| 1-10 oz | can mandarin oranges (or 1 orange, sectioned) | 1-284 mL |
| ½ cup | fresh blueberries | 125 mL |
| ½ lb | seedless green grapes, cut in half | 250 g |
| | fruit sugar to taste | |
| | juice of 2 limes or lemons | |
| ¼ cup | orange liqueur | 50 mL |
| 1 tbsp | rum and/or vodka | 15 mL |

**Cut melons** in half. Remove seeds. Make melon balls or cut flesh in chunks. Trim the pineapple, remove the core and cut in pieces. Toss all the fruit together in a large bowl.

**Sprinkle** with sugar, lime juice, liqueur and rum. Chill for an hour or so, stirring occasionally to let the flavours blend.

**For special** effect, pile the fruit into melon halves or pineapple shells to serve.

**Serves 6**

**Preparing a fresh pineapple:** To test if a pineapple is ripe, pull out a centre leaf. It should come away easily. And take a sniff; the fragrance should be sweet and tropical. Cut the top and bottom from the pineapple. Then trim away the outside skin, working from the top to the bottom. With the tip of a sharp knife, remove the tiny 'eyes'. Slice the pineapple in rounds and remove the centre core (it's usually too tough to eat).

# Fresh Fruit Parfait

This sweet, delicate cream is the base of many simple and spectacular desserts. Particularly delicious with peaches or berries.

| | | |
|---|---|---|
| 4 | eggs, separated | 4 |
| ½ cup | sugar | 125 mL |
| ⅓ cup | flour | 75 mL |
| 2 cups | milk | 500 mL |
| ½ tsp | vanilla | 2 mL |
| 1 tsp | grated orange or lemon rind | 5 mL |
| 1 tbsp | orange liqueur | 15 mL |
| 2 cups | fresh fruit | 500 mL |

**Beat egg** yolks with the sugar in a large bowl until mixture is pale and light. Add flour and mix until smooth.

**Heat milk** in a saucepan and gradually pour hot milk into egg mixture, whisking constantly.

**Return** mixture to saucepan. Cook and stir over medium heat until the sweet cream is smooth and thick. Be patient: it takes a little time but if you cook the sweet cream too quickly it will burn.

**Add vanilla**, orange rind and orange liqueur and pour into a bowl. (A piece of waxed paper placed on the surface will prevent a skin from forming.) Refrigerate until ready to serve.*

**At serving time**, fold fresh fruit, sliced and sprinkled with a little liqueur, into the chilled, sweet cream and pile into individual serving glasses such as wine goblets.

## Serves 6

For a lighter sweet cream, fold in stiffly beaten egg whites.

**Fresh Fruit Tart:** Pile sweet cream into a baked pastry crust and top with fruit.

# Lemon Mousse

Light, refreshing and simple to make.

| | | |
|---|---|---|
| 1½ cups milk | | 375 mL |
| 3 | eggs, separated | 3 |
| 1 tbsp | unflavoured gelatine | 15 mL |
| ½ cup | sugar | 125 mL |
| ½ cup | whipping cream | 125 mL |
| 2 tbsp | lemon juice, plus grated rind | 25 mL |

**Heat milk** to simmer. Combine egg yolks, gelatine, sugar and cream in bowl. Add hot milk. Set bowl over a pan of simmering water. Cook and stir mixture until slightly thickened.

**Add lemon** juice and grated rind. Beat egg whites until stiff and fold into the lemony custard.

**Pour into** a large glass bowl or mold.

**Serves 6**

Delicious served with fresh raspberries or strawberries.

**Orange Wheels:** Peel rind from oranges, 1 per person. (A serrated knife makes this a cinch.) Slice thinly crosswise. Arrange pinwheel fashion in a glass bowl or pie plate. Drizzle with orange liqueur and a sprinkling of honey or sugar. You may also alternate orange slices with pineapple chunks or sliced strawberries, blueberries and a little shredded coconut.

# Topsy Turvy

A basic upside-down cake. Good for kids and grown-ups alike. A quick cake for accidentally forgotten birthdays away from home.

| | | |
|---|---|---|
| 2 tbsp<br>+ ¼ cup | butter | 25 mL<br>+50 mL |
| 1 cup | packed brown sugar | 250 mL |
| 1-19 oz | can sliced pine-<br>apple or peaches,<br>drained | 1-540 mL |
| 1 | egg | 1 |
| ½ cup | milk | 125 mL |
| 1 cup | all-purpose flour | 250 mL |
| 1 tsp | baking powder | 5 mL |
| 1 tsp | vanilla | 5 mL |

**Set oven** to 325°F (160°C).

**Melt** 2 tablespoons (25 mL) butter and ½ cup (125 mL) brown sugar in a 10" (25 cm) cast iron frying pan. Arrange pineapple on top.

**Cream together** remaining butter and sugar. Add the egg and milk.

**Sift together** the flour and baking powder and blend with the other ingredients. Stir in the vanilla. Pour batter over fruit and place pan in oven. Bake 25-30 minutes.

**Remove** from oven and invert on large plate. Watch you don't burn yourself as brown sugar sauce will drip over the sides.

### Serves 6

Cake may also be baked in a glass pie plate.

# Apple Crisp

| ½ tsp | cinnamon | 2 mL |
|---|---|---|
| ½ tsp | cardamom | 2 mL |
| ½ cup | butter | 125 mL |
| ¾ cup | rolled oats | 175 mL |

An old-fashioned dessert, quick and easy to put together and guaranteed to please a sweet-tooth of any age. Use any available fresh fruit, but a sharp fruit such as plums, sour cherries or tart apples is best. Cardamom is a warm spice, excellent with apples, but cinnamon is fine too.

| 8 | cooking apples, peeled, cored and sliced | 8 |
|---|---|---|
| ½ cup | sugar | 125 mL |
| ½ tsp | ground cardamom | 2 mL |
| | juice of ½ lemon | |
| 1 tbsp | butter, melted | 15 mL |

**Topping:**

| ½ cup | flour | 125 mL |
|---|---|---|
| ½ cup | packed brown sugar | 125 mL |
| | pinch salt | |

**Set oven** to 350°F (180°C).

**Toss fruit** with sugar, cardamom, lemon juice and butter and spread in an 8" x 8" (2 L) shallow baking dish.

**Combine** flour, sugar, salt, cinnamon and cardamom for topping. Cut in butter with two knives or a pastry blender until mixture resembles coarse crumbs. Mix in rolled oats and spread topping over fruit.

**Bake** about 40 minutes.

**Serves 6**

Wonderful with vanilla-flavoured whipped cream.

**Preparing whipped cream ahead:**
Add 1 teaspoon gelatin (5 mL) to ¼ cup (50 mL) cold water. Set over hot water and stir until dissolved. Cool slightly. Stir into whipping cream and beat in the normal way. Refrigerate.

# Plum Cake

Top the sweet crust with any fresh fruit you have on hand and serve with lashings of lightly sweetened whipped cream.

| | | |
|---|---|---|
| 2 lbs | plums | 1 kg |
| 1 cup | all-purpose flour | 250 mL |
| 1 cup | sugar | 250 mL |
| 1 tsp | baking powder | 5 mL |
| | pinch salt | |
| ¼ cup | butter | 50 mL |
| 1 | egg, beaten | 1 |
| 1 tsp | vanilla | 5 mL |

### Topping:

| | | |
|---|---|---|
| 3 tbsp | sugar | 45 mL |
| 3 tbsp | melted butter | 45 mL |
| 1 tsp | cinnamon | 5 mL |
| 1 | egg, beaten | 1 |

**Set oven** to 350°F (180°C).

**Cut plums** in half and remove stones.

**Combine** flour, sugar, baking powder and salt in a large bowl.

**Cut butter** into flour mixture with two knives or a pastry blender until mixture resembles coarse crumbs.

**Add egg** and vanilla and toss all together.

**Spread** crust mixture in a 9" (23 cm) pie plate and pat down. Lay fruit on top.

**Bake** 40 minutes.

**Combine** topping ingredients, spoon on top of cake and continue baking about 20 minutes longer, until topping is set and lightly browned.

**Serves 6**

# Cheddar/Apple Pie

For those who hate making pies.

| | | |
|---|---|---|
| 1 tbsp | brown sugar | 15 mL |
| 1 tsp | cinnamon | 5 mL |
| 1 tsp | grated lemon rind | 5 mL |
| 4 | tart apples, peeled, cored and sliced | 4 |
| 1 | Cheddar Cheese Crust | 1 |

**Set oven** to 350°F (180°C).

**Toss together** the sugar, cinnamon, lemon rind and apple slices.

**Press** about ⅔ of the Cheddar crust into a greased 9" (23 cm) pie plate. Top with apple slices and sprinkle with remaining crumb mixture.

**Bake** until crust is crisp and apples are tender (approximately 30-40 minutes). If you can wait, let cool until just warm before slicing.

**Serve with** a scoop of ice cream or a good spoonful of whipped cream.

**Serves 6**

These make great bars as well. Simply use a 9" x 13" (3 L) glass baking dish to assemble in. Cool before cutting.

## Cheddar Cheese Crust

The crust is like making a giant cookie. You can't ruin it.

| | | |
|---|---|---|
| 1 cup | flour | 250 mL |
| ½ cup | sugar | 125 mL |
| ½ cup | rolled oats | 125 mL |
| ½ cup | butter | 125 mL |
| 1 cup | grated Cheddar cheese | 250 mL |

**Combine flour**, sugar and oats. Blend in the butter and cheese. (All the ingredients may be thrown together in food processor to blend.)

# Key Lime Pie

This is a northern Georgian Bay favourite

| | | |
|---|---|---|
| 1 | Graham Cracker Crust | 1 |
| 4 | eggs, separated | 4 |
| 1-10 oz | can condensed milk | 1-300 mL |
| ½ cup | lime juice | 125 mL |
| 6 tbsp | sugar | 100 mL |
| | pinch of salt | |

**Set oven** to 350°F (180°C).

**Beat egg yolks** in a large bowl until creamy. Add condensed milk and lime juice and beat until thick and smooth. Beat 1 egg white until stiff and fold into lime mixture.

**Pour into** prebaked pie shell. Beat remaining egg whites and salt until stiff.

**Sprinkle with** sugar and continue beating until mixture holds firm peaks. Spread over pie filling.

**Bake** 10-15 minutes, until lightly browned. Chill before serving.

### Serves 6

**Lime Parfait:** Prepare lime custard filling for Key Lime Pie. Beat all the egg whites with the sugar and fold into the lime mixture. Spoon into wine glasses and chill. Serve with fresh fruit.

**Graham Cracker Crust:** Crush 4 ounces (100 g) graham wafers or zwieback to make 1¼ cups (300 mL) crumbs. Combine with ¼ cup (50 mL) sugar and ¼ cup (50 mL) melted butter. Add a pinch of cinnamon or grated nutmeg if you fancy a spicy crust. Press mixture evenly over bottom and sides of a 9" (23 cm) pie plate. Bake at 375°F (190°C) 8 minutes. Cool.

# Deep Dish Pie

The kind bears like to steal from porches, especially the harmless two-legged variety.

| | | |
|---|---|---|
| 4 to 6 cups | fruit (enough to fill pie shell) | 1-1.5 L |
| ½ cup | sugar | 125 mL |
| 2 tbsp | flour | 25 mL |
| ½ tsp | cinnamon | 2 mL |
| ½ tsp | nutmeg | 2 mL |
| 1 tbsp | lemon juice | 15 mL |
| 3 tbsp | butter | 45 mL |
| | double pastry crust (page 182) | |

**Set oven** to 350°F (180°C).

**Lightly butter** a 9" (23 cm) pie plate.

**Wash fruit**, peel and slice if necessary. Combine the sugar, flour, cinnamon and nutmeg. Toss with the fruit. If your fruit is really juicy add an extra tablespoon (15 mL) flour.

**Roll out** slightly less than ½ of the pastry on a floured board and fit into pie dish.

**Heap fruit** mixture into crust. Drizzle with lemon juice and dot with butter. Roll out remaining pastry dough and lay gently on top. Trim extra pastry and press the edges with the tines of a fork to seal. Make small slits in top of the crust. Bake 40 minutes.

**Serves 6**

This pie is most delicious when eaten warm, even if the fruit does run all over the place.

**The finishing touch to fruit pies:** Ten minutes before the pie is ready, brush crust with cream, sprinkle with sugar and return to oven.

# Rum Tart

A chocolate wafer crust makes this pie a snap.

| | | |
|---|---|---|
| 1 | Chocolate Wafer Crust | 1 |
| 6 | egg yolks | 6 |
| 1 cup | sugar | 250 mL |
| 1 tbsp | unflavoured gelatine | 15 mL |
| ½ cup | cold water | 125 mL |
| 1 cup | whipping cream | 250 mL |
| ⅓ cup | rum | 75 mL |
| 2-1 oz | squares semi-sweet chocolate | 2-28 g |

**Beat egg** yolks with sugar until very light, smooth and pale yellow.

**Soften gelatine** in cold water. Place in a bowl over a pan of hot water and stir to dissolve. Gradually beat the gelatine into the egg mixture.

**Beat cream** until stiff and fold into the eggs along with the rum. Pour into the crust.

**Shred chocolate** on top and refrigerate overnight, or freeze.

**Serves 6 to 8**

For a really impressive look, arrange a few well-drained maraschino cherries with stems on top before serving.

**Chocolate Wafer Crust:** Crush a 7-ounce (200 g) package chocolate wafers between 2 sheets of waxed paper with a rolling pin, or whirl them briefly in a blender, to make 2 cups crumbs. Combine with ¼ cup (50 mL) melted butter. Spread mixture evenly over bottom and sides of a 9" (23 cm) pie plate. Chill until needed.

# Winter Fruit Compote

| | | |
|---|---|---|
| ½ cup | sugar | 125 mL |
| 1 cup | water | 250 mL |
| | juice and grated rind of 1 lemon | |
| 1 | cinnamon stick | 1 |
| 1-6 oz | mixed dried fruit | 1-170 g |
| 1 tbsp | brandy (optional) | 15 mL |

**Combine sugar**, water, lemon juice and rind and cinnamon stick in a small pot. Bring to a boil and stir until sugar is dissolved.

**Stir in** the dried fruit and cook over low heat 20-25 minutes, until fruit is softened.

**Stir in** brandy. Spoon hot over ice cream or serve chilled in wine glasses.

**Makes 2 to 4 servings**

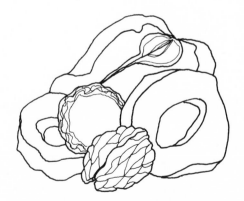

# Thirst Quenchers

**W**e have simple drinking tastes but now and again madness takes over. Of course, it's the fault of friends who show up with a bottle of Jack Daniel's and a bunch of mint or the makings of a margarita.

For occasions like these, we include some well-researched concoctions for the amateur bartender. Some are long and cool to quench a thirst, others are warm and spicy to lend comfort on chilly evenings. Some are served at the happy hour, others take the place of an after-dinner mint.

# Eye openers

...this time she found a little bottle.. with the words 'DRINK ME' beautifully printed on it... Alice ventured to taste it, and finding it very nice (it had, in fact, a sort of mixed flavour of cherry-tart, custard, pineapple, roast turkey, toffy, and hot buttered toast), she very soon finished it off.
*Alice in Wonderland,*
*Lewis Carroll*

## The Ultimate Bloody Mary

Quantities for one, which won't be enough!

| | | |
|---|---|---|
| ½ | fresh lime | ½ |
| | celery salt | |
| 1½ oz | vodka | 45 mL |
| 6 oz | tomato juice | 175 mL |
| ½ tsp | horseradish | 2 mL |
| | Tabasco and Worcestershire sauce to taste | |
| | salt | |
| | freshly ground pepper | |
| | ice cubes | |
| | lime wedges | |
| | celery stalks | |

**Rub rim** of glass with cut lime and dip in celery salt.

**Combine** vigorously vodka, tomato juice, horseradish, Tabasco, Worcestershire sauce, salt and pepper.

**Pour over** ice in prepared glass. Add a lime wedge after giving it a squeeze. Stir and serve with a celery stalk.

**Makes 1**

## Sure Cure

Good for whatever ails you.

| | | |
|---|---|---|
| 1 oz | vodka | 30 mL |
| 3 oz | strong beef bouillion | 90 mL |
| 2 oz | tomato juice | 60 mL |
| | squeeze lemon juice | |
| | salt and freshly ground pepper | |

**Mix** and serve very cold.

**Makes 1**

# Happy Hour

## Mint Julep

| | | |
|---|---|---:|
| | a bunch of fresh mint | |
| 1 tsp | sugar | 5 mL |
| 2 tsp | water | 10 mL |
| | bourbon | |
| | finely crushed ice | |

**Crush** a few mint leaves with the sugar and water in the bottom of a frosted goblet or glass. Pour bourbon to the halfway mark and fill glass with ice. Gently stir.

**Toss** a few mint leaves on top, tearing them a little to release the minty aromas.

### Makes 1

**Crushed ice country-style:** Place ice cubes in a tough large plastic bag and wrap in a towel. Whack package repeatedly with a hammer.

## Piña Colada

For very lazy summer afternoons; when someone else is doing the cooking. Use Coco Lopez brand cream of coconut for best results.

| | | |
|---|---|---:|
| 3 oz | cream of coconut | 90 mL |
| 6 oz | pineapple juice | 175 mL |
| 4 oz | rum | 125 mL |
| | squirt lemon or lime juice | |
| 8 | ice cubes | 8 |
| 4 | maraschino cherries | 4 |
| | freshly grated nutmeg | |

**Blend all** ingredients, except the cherries and nutmeg, in a blender.

**Pour into** frosted glasses. Top each with a cherry and a sprinkle of nutmeg.

### Makes 4

## Margarita

A south-of-the-border taste even when you are sitting on northern shores.

| 1-2 | lime | 1-2 |
|-----|------|-----|
| | salt | |
| 1 oz | orange liqueur | 30 mL |
| 1 oz | tequila | 30 mL |
| | ice finely crushed | |

**Rub rim** of a frosted wine glass with a cut lime and dip in salt. Combine 1 oz (30 mL) lime juice, orange liqueur and tequila. Pour over crushed ice.

**Makes 1**

## Cancún Margarita

Good after a long stroll on a sandy beach.

| | salt | |
|-----|------|-----|
| 1 | lime | 1 |
| 1 oz | tequila | 30 mL |
| | grapefruit juice | |
| | ice cubes | |

**Rub rim** of a tall frosted glass with a cut lime and dip in salt.

**Fill glass** with ice. Add the tequila and top with grapefruit juice. Add a lime wedge after giving it a good squeeze first.

**Makes 1**

## Banana Daiquiri

A snack in itself.

| | | |
|---|---|---|
| 1 | ripe banana | 1 |
| 6 oz | rum | 175 mL |
| ½ cup | lime juice | 125 mL |
| 1 tsp | sugar | 5 mL |
| 8 | ice cubes | 8 |

**Peel** and slice banana.

**Place** in blender jar with other ingredients and whirl until thick and smooth. Pour into chilled wine glasses.

**Makes 4**

**Summer coolers:** On really hot days, if you have room, keep your bottles of gin and tonic in the fridge. The ice will then melt more slowly and your drink will be cold, refreshing and not diluted.

## Spritzer

A spritzer is light and refreshing on a summer afternoon. Pour about 6 ounces (175 mL) chilled fruity, dry, white wine into a large wine glass. Add a couple of ice cubes. Top up with chilled soda water and add a twist of lemon.

**Frosted glasses:** Cooling drinks on hot, lazy days are extra refreshing served in frosted glasses. Stick glasses in the freezer at least 30 minutes ahead of time. Take them out as you need them.

**Keep cool:** Often the best refrigerator for beer or wine is a shady spot in a cold stream or lake. In winter, just stick a bottle or two in a snow bank. If you don't have snow, fill your sink with ice cubes and water. Wine or beer will be chilled within minutes.

# The Comfort Cup

## Spiced Tea

A heartwarming brew. Try loose leaf Ceylonese tea; it has a marvellous fragrance.

| | | |
|---|---|---|
| 2 tsp | tea | 10 mL |
| 1 | 3" piece cinnamon stick | 1 |
| 2 | whole cloves | 2 |
| 1 cup | boiling water | 250 mL |
| 1 cup | hot milk | 250 mL |
| 1 tsp | honey | 5 mL |

**Toss tea** and spices into a warm pot and pour in boiling water.

**Brew** 5 minutes and strain into a pitcher.

**Add hot milk** and sweeten with honey to taste.

**Serves 2**

## Hot Chocolate

No better way to block out chilly temperatures from both mind and body.

| | | |
|---|---|---|
| 1 tbsp | Chocolate Sauce (page 192) | 15 mL |
| 1 cup | hot milk | 250 mL |
| 1 | cinnamon stick | 1 |

**Blend chocolate** sauce into hot milk and stir with a cinnamon stick.

**Makes 1**

Children like a topping of marshmallows. Adults may prefer a dash of Tia Maria or a little Bailey's Original Irish Cream.

**Chilly Chocolate Milk:** Blend Chocolate Sauce (page 192) into cold milk and serve over ice cubes.

## Mulled Wine

A soothing, warming drink; just multiply the quantities to serve a large group.

| | | |
|---|---|---|
| 1 35-oz | bottle full-bodied red wine | 1 L |
| | rind of 1 lemon | |
| 1 | whole nutmeg, crushed (optional) | 1 |
| | a few cloves | |
| 1 | cinnamon stick | 1 |
| | sugar to taste | |

**Toss** all ingredients in a large pot. Stir over medium heat until almost to the boiling point. Ladle into warm mugs.

### Serves 4

Add ½ cup (125 mL) brandy to the mixture for added warmth.

## Cider Bowl

A cozy drink for chilly evenings.

| | | |
|---|---|---|
| 4 cups | apple cider | 1 L |
| 1 | orange, sliced | 1 |
| 8 | whole cloves | 8 |
| 2 | 3" pieces cinnamon stick | 2 |
| | brown sugar | |
| ½ cup | dark rum | 125 mL |

**Combine** cider, orange slices, cloves and cinnamon in a saucepan. Bruise the orange slices to release the juice. Bring to a boil, reduce heat to low and simmer about 10 minutes.

**Remove orange** and spices. Add sugar to taste. Stir in rum.

**Serve** in mugs with a cinnamon stick and an orange slice.

### Serves 4

# Thirst Quenchers

## Sangria

The flavours are at their most seductive if they have a few hours, or overnight, in which to mingle.

| | | |
|---|---|---|
| 1 | orange | 1 |
| 1 | lemon, sliced | 1 |
| 1 | peach, peeled and sliced | 1 |
| 1-24 oz | bottle light red wine | 750 mL |
| 1½ oz | cognac | 45 mL |
| 1 oz | orange liqueur | 30 mL |
| 1 oz | maraschino cherry juice | 30 mL |
| 1 tbsp | sugar | 15 mL |
| 6 oz | soda water | 175 mL |
| 12 | ice cubes | 12 |

**Cut rind** from the orange carefully in one long coil, leaving the orange still attached at the end. Cut away the pith (the white inner skin) at the same time. Do this over a pitcher to catch the juice.

**Combine lemon** and peach slices, wine, cognac, orange liqueur, maraschino juice and sugar in the pitcher.

**Hook orange** peel over the rim of the jug and suspend the orange in the wine mixture. Leave to marinate overnight.

**Before serving**, stir in soda and ice.

**Serves 4**

## The Shandy Jug

The ultimate in thirst quenchers.

Fill a large jug with ice cubes. Add cold beer and ginger beer in the ratio of 2 to 1.

## Blackcurrant Sparkle

|       | ice cubes          |       |
| ----- | ------------------ | ----- |
| 1 oz  | blackcurrant syrup | 30 mL |
|       | lemon slice        |       |
|       | soda water         |       |
|       | fresh mint         |       |

**Fill** tall glass with ice. Add blackcurrant syrup and a squeeze of lemon. Drop lemon slice into glass and top with soda.

## Grapefruit Fizz

Combine unsweetened grapefruit juice and soda water to taste in a tall glass with lots of ice. Add a good squeeze and twist of fresh lime.

## Orange Fizz

Combine orange juice and soda water to taste in a tall glass with lots of ice. Flavour with orange and lime slices and a sprig of fresh mint.

## Princess Leah

For those too young for Shirley Temples.

|        |                  |        |
| ------ | ---------------- | ------ |
| 1 tbsp | grenadine syrup  | 15 mL  |
| 4 oz   | orange juice     | 125 mL |
| 4 oz   | ginger ale       | 125 mL |
|        | ice cubes        |        |
| 1      | maraschino cherry | 1     |
| 1      | orange slice     | 1      |

**Combine** grenadine, orange juice and ginger ale. Pour over ice in a tall glass. Top with a cherry.

**Serve with** colourful straws and a slice of orange.

**Makes 1**

**From our experience:** Why is it that no matter how well you stock the fridge, *someone else* always gets the last beer or glass of lemonade?

# After the Feast

## Irish Coffee

Always be prepared to make seconds.

| | | |
|---|---|---|
| 1 cup | whipping cream | 250 mL |
| 1 tbsp | brandy | 15 mL |
| 1 | lemon, halved | 1 |
| ¼ cup | sugar | 50 mL |
| 4 tsp | instant coffee | 20 mL |
| 4 tsp | brown sugar | 20 mL |
| | hot water | |
| 4 oz | Irish whiskey | 120 mL |
| | freshly grated nutmeg | |

**Before making** Irish Coffee, assemble all ingredients and 4 tempered glasses.

**Beat** the whipping cream until it is thick but will still pour slowly.

**Warm brandy** in a small pot. Divide between 2 of the tempered glasses. Set a match to the brandy and carefully pour it, still flaming, into the 2 empty glasses. Swirl to warm the glasses. Hot water also works, but isn't much fun.

**Rub rim** of each glass with lemon juice and dip upside down in sugar (fruit sugar is best).

**Place** 1 teaspoon (5 mL) instant coffee and brown sugar in each glass. Add a little hot water and stir to dissolve; or use strong freshly brewed coffee. Pour in 1 ounce (30 mL) Irish whiskey. Top with hot water to ½" (1.25 cm) from the rim.

**Pour** whipped cream gently over the back of a spoon to fill each glass. Sprinkle with a little grated nutmeg.

**Makes 4**

## Cappuccino

A delicious substitute when you can't get the real thing.

| | | |
|---|---|---|
| 1 cup | whipping cream | 250 mL |
| 2 cups | milk | 500 mL |
| 1 cup | very strong coffee | 250 mL |
| | sugar to taste | |
| | cinnamon | |

**Beat** ¾ cup (200 mL) whipping cream until stiff.

**Heat milk** and remaining ¼ cup (50 mL) cream in a small saucepan. Add the coffee and sugar. Stir to blend.

**Pour** into mugs or tempered glasses. Spoon whipped cream on top and sprinkle with cinnamon.

**Serves 4**

## Grenada Coffee

Ice-cold coffee, spiked with a variety of liqueurs (omit those with a fruit base), makes a superb dessert.

| | | |
|---|---|---|
| | ice cubes | |
| 4 oz | coffee-flavoured liqueur | 125 mL |
| | strong freshly brewed coffee | |
| | table cream to taste | |
| | sugar to taste | |
| | freshly grated nutmeg | |

**Fill glasses** (large wine glasses work well) with lots of ice.

**Add** 1 ounce (30 mL) liqueur to each glass. Top with hot coffee.

**Add cream** and sugar, and sprinkle with freshly grated nutmeg.

**Makes 4**

# Ughs & Yuks

The name says it all. This isn't serious food but a few of those sweet, awful, marvellous treats, like gooey toasted marshmallows smothered in chocolate, which make nutritionists throw up their arms in dismay and food purists shudder. They are quick, easy and fun to make and most of us find them irresistible.

# Happy Birthday to You

*As cooks go, she went.*
*H.H. Munro*

August birthdays mean yet another minnow pail, or six cleats for the dock or, if you're lucky, a *new* muskie killer. So why not a birthday cake of the adult ugh and yuk variety?

| | | |
|---|---|---|
| 1 | Chocolate Wafer Crust (page 202) | 1 |
| 30 | large marshmallows | 30 |
| ½ cup | milk | 125 mL |
| ⅓ cup | crème de menthe | 75 mL |
| 1 cup | whipping cream, whipped | 250 mL |
| | grated dark chocolate (optional) | |

**Prepare** Chocolate Wafer Crust.

**Melt marshmallows** with milk in a small saucepan over low heat. Let cool to room temperature.

**Stir liqueur** into marshmallow mixture and gently fold in whipped cream.

**Pour** into pie shell and sprinkle with grated chocolate.

**Refrigerate** until chilled or cover and freeze.

**Serve** chilled or frozen.

**Serves 6 to 8**

---

**Tip:** Use sparklers instead of candles on adult birthday cakes: the numbers aren't significant and they blow themselves out.

# Mud Pie

Take one large pail of sand. Mix carefully with a quart of water. Pat well to shape into a large pie. Or try the following:

| | | |
|---|---|---|
| 1 | Chocolate Wafer Crust (page 202) | 1 |
| 1 quart | vanilla ice cream | 1 L |
| 1 cup | Chocolate Sauce, cooled (page 192) | 250 mL |
| 1 cup | whipping cream | 250 mL |
| | a peanut or two or three or four..... | |

**Mash ice cream** to soften and spoon into the pie shell. Swirl chocolate sauce on top and slip into freezer.

**When ready** to serve, pile high with whipped cream and sprinkle with peanuts. UGH! YUK!

**Serves 6**

# S'Mores

A sweet, sticky marshmallow sandwich; a camper's treat.

| | | |
|---|---|---|
| 1 | large marshmallow | 1 |
| 2 | graham crackers | 2 |
| 1 | dark chocolate | 1 |

**Toast** a marshmallow until lightly golden all over. This requires no mean skill, concentration and patience, as well as a fire that has burned down to glowing embers. (Some people, of course, prefer their marshmallows charred to a cinder; the ones that fall off the stick and end up stuck to the bottom of everyone's running shoes and on the dog's feet.)

**Fix the hot**, gluey mess on a graham cracker and lay a piece of chocolate bar on top—it melts instantly. Top with another graham cracker.

**Makes 1**

# O'Henry Bars

The name speaks for itself. Keep stored in a cool place.

| | | |
|---|---|---|
| 1/3 cup | butter | 75 mL |
| ½ cup | brown sugar | 125 mL |
| ¼ cup | light corn syrup | 50 mL |
| 1 tsp | vanilla | 5 mL |
| 2 cups | rolled oats | 500 mL |
| 3-1 oz | squares semi-sweet chocolate | 3-28 g |
| 1/3 cup | peanut butter | 75 mL |
| ½ cup | chopped peanuts | 125 mL |

**Set oven** to 350°F (180°C).

**Cream together** the butter and sugar. Stir in the corn syrup, vanilla and rolled oats. Spread in a lightly ground 8" x 8" (2L) baking pan. Bake 15 minutes.

**Remove** from oven and cool. Melt chocolate and peanut butter together. Spread over base. Sprinkle with peanuts. Chill before cutting into squares.

**Makes 16 2-inch (5 cm) bars**

# Kid's Stuff

Chewy, gooey and wonderful.

| | | |
|---|---|---|
| ½ cup | butter | 125 mL |
| 1½ cups | graham cracker crumbs | 375 mL |
| 1-10 oz | can sweetened condensed milk | 1-300 mL |
| 1 cup | chocolate chips | 250 mL |
| 1¼ cups | unsweetened desiccated coconut | 300 mL |
| 1 cup | chopped walnuts or peanuts | 250 mL |

**Set oven** to 350°F (180°C).

**Melt butter** in a 9″ x 13″ (3 L) pan in oven.

**Spread crumbs** evenly over butter and pour condensed milk evenly on top of crumbs. Sprinkle with remaining ingredients and press down firmly.

**Bake** 25-30 minutes, until lightly browned, taking care that the bottom does not burn.

**Cool** and cut into squares.

**Makes 24 2-inch (5 cm) bars**

# INDEX